My Original Ambition

Letters from persons of consequence

by

Dominic Shelmerdine

To: Paul Keylock.
Thank You so much for your
help. — All Best Wishes
[signature]
December 2004.

Published by D. S. Publishing
PO Box 36176
London
SW7 4YW

Printed and bound in Great Britain.

ISBN 0 9548279 0 2

A CIP Catalogue record for this book is available from the British Library.

for Sebastian

Acknowledgements

Janan Barbar
Kay Cahill
Hazel Cook
Ursula Davisson
Huriy Ghirmai
Anna Gogacz
Elaine Goh
Woody Goldberg
Jonathan Hellewell
Gillian Hennessey
Jane N. M. Hodgkinson
Francis Hutchison
Paul Keylock
Igor Korchilov
Igor Krasnovski
Lizzie Lawrence
Jean-Loup Lopez
Linda Mahler
Natalia Marin

Alexander A. Masson
Christine McAteer
Godwin Mfula
Dawn Merck
Pilar Navarro
Miroslawa Odish
Gina Page
Pavel Palazchenko
Maria J. Perez
José Perez Zamora
Vladimir Polyakov
John Plummer
Jill Saunders
John V. Schneider-Merck
Guy L. Shelmerdine
Wojciech Skawski
Robert J. W. Smith
Jan Vulevich
Phyliss Whiting

Foreword

Have you ever wondered what the original ambitions of some of the world's leading personalities might have been? Did they really aspire to become president, prime minister, Hollywood film star, premiership footballer or world golfing champion, etc? Much has been written about the persons of consequence within these pages – either biographical or autobiographical as can be found in book shops, libraries or via the internet. Little, if anything however, is known of their earliest ambitions. I decided to find out and over the course of thirteen years, several thousand hand-written letters of invitation were issued, hundreds of telephone calls and faxes made and sent. In the majority of cases, invitees returned polite refusals or simply failed to respond at all. Diplomacy, negotiation and patience were required in abundance from the outset. Finally, enough interesting material was acquired to produce this book. Reproduced herein are the exact replies, as received – all personally signed. Hopefully, the reader will enjoy the contents of this compilation as much as the writer did in receiving them.

Dominic Shelmerdine
London 2004

The Daily Telegraph

181 MARSH WALL LONDON E14 9SR
TELEPHONE: 071-538 5000   TELEX: 22874 TELLDN G

DIRECT LINE: 071-538 6301/6312   FAX: 071-538 3810

FROM THE EDITOR   14 March 1991

Dr Mr. Shelmerdine,

For a brief period in my early years, I wanted
to be a soldier. By the time I was 16, I knew
I wanted to be a writer and journalist like my
parents. Since then, my enthusiasm has never wavered.

Y—,

THE DAILY TELEGRAPH PLC REGISTERED IN ENGLAND No. 451593 REGISTERED OFFICE AS ABOVE

Dear Dominic Shelmerdine —
I send you my very
best wishes and I hope that
book is a great, wonderful
success.

Sincerely James Stewart

18 March 1991.

Dear Dominic,

Thank you for your letter of 11 March 1991.

In answer to your question I can say that my original ambition in life was to become a Member of Parliament.

I achieved this on 23 February 1950 and I have now been an M.P. continuously for forty one years.

With best wishes.

Yours sincerely,

Edward Heath

HOUSE OF COMMONS
LONDON SW1A 0AA

19th March, 1991.

Dear Mr. Shelmerdine,

      Thank you for your letter of the 11th March. My first
ambition was to play cricket for England, but it soon became
clear that that was out of my reach. After that, I have no
fixed ambition, save a desire to lead an interesting and useful
life, which on the whole I have managed to do.

      Yours sincerely,

From: Dame Barbara Cartland, D.B.E., D.St.J.

POTTERS BAR (0707)
42612
42657
FAX: 0707 42640

CAMFIELD PLACE,
HATFIELD,
HERTFORDSHIRE.
AL9 6JE

21st March 1991.

Dear Mr. Shelmerdine,

Thank you so much for your letter.

My Mother always brought us up
to believe that the most valuable thing
you could give, was of yourself!

She said that any fool who had money
in the Bank could write a cheque, but what
really mattered was what you personally gave
to other people.

The moment I began to write I felt
I had to give Beauty and Love to people.
Now I have jsut finished my 537th book.

I do hope that your book is a
huge success.

With all best wishes,

Love John Cartland

HOUSE OF COMMONS
LONDON SW1A 0AA

21st March 1991

Dear Mr Shelmerdine,

Thank you for your letter. My original
ambitions were to play football like Tom
Finney, the star player for my favourite football team Preston North End and to go into the
Church as a Clergyman. I finished up playing
rugby and being a politician!

Kindest regards.

Yours sincerely,

Dominic Shelmerdine Esq.

HOUSE OF COMMONS
LONDON SW1A 0AA

CS/IY   22nd March 1991

Dear Mr Shelmerdine

Thank you for your letter dated 19th March 1991.

My earliest ambition in life was to become Mayor of
Rochdale - and I achieved it.

My second was to be a millionaire and go around giving
money to people in need.   That one I did **NOT** achieve.

Yours sincerely

SIR CYRIL SMITH   MBE DL
Member of Parliament

House of Lords

The Rt. Hon. The Lord Wilson of Rievaulx KG OBE FRS

25 March, 1991

Dear Mr. Shelmerdine,

Thank you for your letter of
the 16 March.

I was interested to know of the
book you are compiling.

My original ambition was to be
Chancellor of the Exchequer and to introduce more
Budgets than William Gladstone. It was a very early
ambition from primary school days. As you will see,
I always wanted to be in politics and Parliament.

With every good wish,

Yours sincerely,

Wilson of Rievaulx

Dominic Shelmerdine

26 March 1991

Dear Dominic

Thank you for your request about top peoples original ambitions.

My original ambition in life was to be a Band Leader. My heroes
were Jack Hylton and Billy Cotton. Unfortunately I am not as
musical as I had hoped to be; but leading the Church of England
is a bit like keeping a variety of sound sections under control.

Yours sincerely

The Rt Revd Lord Runcie

"Gable End"
22, Dorney Reach Road,
Dorney Reach,
Maidenhead,
SL6 0DX.

March 27th 1991.

Dear Dominic.

Thanks for your letter of the 23rd of March.

My father worked on the railway as a signal lampman.

So my ambition was to become a train driver they
earned over 10 pounds a week.

Other than that I loved cricket and airoplanes
so it was either a cricketer or pilot.

In the long run Ive been very happy as an entertainer
I think thats my vocation.

My one dissapointment was I never learned the piano.
because Im a natural song and dance man and very
musical.

All the Best

Ernie Wise OBE.

27 Mar: 91

Dear Mr Shelmerdine : Thank you for yr: letter
So far back as I can remember I have
always wished to be called to the Bar, to
serve in public life, and, if the need arose,
to fight for my country. All these ambitions
have been granted me. LAUS DEO.

Hailsham

MENCAP

Royal Society for Mentally Handicapped
Children and Adults

Mencap National Centre
123 Golden Lane
London EC1Y 0RT
Tel: 071-454 0454
Fax: 071-608 3254

Patron HM Queen Elizabeth The Queen Mother

President The Lord Allen of Abbeydale GCB
Chairman Sir Brian Rix CBE DL
Senior Director Fred Heddell

BR/NG/mvr

28 March 1991

Dear Dominic Shelmerdine

Thank you for your letter of 19 March.

My original ambition, as a child, was quite simple: To be a
famous cricketer, a famous doctor or a famous actor. At
least I partially achieved my final ambition!

Only years later did it occur to me to try to become the
Secretary-General of Mencap. This I did in 1980, followed
by the Chairmanship of the Royal Society in 1988. I am a
very lucky man.

I hope that gives you all the information you need.

Yours sincerely

Chairman

Past President The Rt. Hon. Lord Renton KBE TD QC Vice-Presidents The Rt. Hon. The Lord Broxbourne QC
His Grace The Archbishop of Canterbury (President of British Council of Churches)
Mrs Judy Fryd MBE Mrs Pauline Fairbrother Mr Neville Thompson Mr Helmut Rothenberg OBE
Hon. Treasurer Mr Barrie Davis
Aims To increase public awareness and understanding of the problems of people with a mental
handicap so as to secure provision for them commensurate with their needs.
Registered as a charity in accordance with the National Assistance Act 1948 and the Charities Act 1960
Company Reg. No. 550457 (England)

18

CLIFF MICHELMORE

Bembridge, Isle of Wight
1st April 1991

Dear Dominic,

As I entered my early teens I had
the idea that I could play professional
cricket and football as a sideline to
being a farmer.

In the end I joined the Royal Air Force
then went on to the British Forces
Network in Germany   , left the RAF and
somehow got involved in   television.

I never did become a farmer although
I did play sport with a modicum of
success and a great deal of enjoyment.
So much for the stuff that dreams are
made on ....

Good Luck with the book
Cliff Michelmore

National Spinal Injuries Centre

Jimmy Savile Stoke Mandeville
Hospital Trust, No. 283127
Jimmy Savile Charitable Trust,
No. 326970

at Stoke Mandeville Hospital

Mandeville Road Aylesbury Bucks HP21 8AL   Tel: Aylesbury (0296) 84111

Date   2.4.91   Please reply to:-

Dear Dominic,

All I ever wanted to be was loaded and having nothing
to do. It only took about 30 years!

Yours sincerely,

SIR JAMES SAVILE KT., OBE., KCSG

20

House of Lords

The Baroness Falkender, CBE

2 April, 1991

Dear Mr. Shelmerdine,

Thank you for your letter of the 23 March.

My original ambition was always to work in Parliament in some way. I was always interested in history, particularly modern political history, and indeed I read history at university. Equally I wanted to see greater fairness and justice for all in society and thought it best to aim for Pariament, though not as an MP.

I do have to confess, however, that before secondary school, at about the age of eight, I wanted to work in a shoe shop. I loved the smell of new leather.

With best wishes,

Yours sincerely,

Marie Falkender

Dominic Shelmerdine, Esq.

Claude Cheysson,
Député au Parlement européen.   Paris, April 2, 1991.

Dear Dominic Shelmerdine,

I refer to your letter dated March 25 and feel most honoured you consider I am one of the « 100 top people » who should tell you of their « original ambitions in life ».

I am not sure you should address French men or women of my generation ; at the time of our first ambitions, we were mostly, if not only, concerned with occupation and war. I myself was still very young when the Germans occupied France ; my only ambition then was that they should be defeated, all the more as the three brothers of my mother had been killed during World War I and my only brother had been shot down as an Air Force officer in June 40.

This « original ambition » was met in 1944-1945 ; and I could contribute to the liberation of my country, coming back from England as a tank officer in the Free French Forces.

Later, other ambitions came. But I undrestand your book bears only on the « original » ones.

Yours sincerely.

C. Cheysson .

DAVID JACOBS

Dear Dominic,

For several years of my childhood I spent
my summer holidays on a farm at Hoath near
Canterbury, six glorious weeks every summer.
I was there the summer of '39 when war broke
out and I stayed on and went to the local
school. I would get up early in the morning,
fetch in the cows, feed the chickens and
collect the eggs before the school bus arrived.

When it brought me back I was there in time
for the afternoon milking. I had my own
stool, my own pail and my own white cap. I
remember with pleasure putting my forehead on
the warm flank of the favourite Jersey cow
and hearing the first 'sing' as her milk
spurted into a bucket. A farmer was what I
would be. I might have been and probably
never will but it's a cosy thought.

Yours sincerely,

DAVID JACOBS

FROM THE CHAIRMAN, MARMADUKE HUSSEY

BRITISH BROADCASTING CORPORATION
BROADCASTING HOUSE
LONDON W1A 1AA
TELEPHONE: 071-580 4468
TELEX: 265781

3rd April 1991

Thank you very much for your letter, asking for my original ambitions in life.

I am afraid my early life was dominated by sport, as I was lucky enough to come from a sporting family. My great-uncle played cricket for England against Australia; several of my relations had played cricket for Oxford or Cambridge; and my father ran for Oxford and also in the Olympics in 1908. And so my first major ambition was to try to emulate them, primarily in cricket or rugby football, both of which I enjoyed and played for Rugby School and Oxford in 1941/42.

When I started to think about careers, my ambition was to join the Diplomatic Service, which was then regarded as the most difficult and most exciting of all the Services. However when the time came in 1949 to consider taking up a job, my health was unsuitable for the constant travel and varied weather of that Service, so on the spur of the moment, having never thought of it before (although I had always been an avid reader) I joined the newspaper industry.

It never occured to me to join the BBC until I was asked, years later.

With all good wishes

Marmaduke Hussey

Jeffrey Archer

3rd April 1991

Dear Mr Skelmersdine,

Many thanks for your letter of 18th March.

My original ambition in life was to be a soldier, thus
following my father. I would have liked to have joined the
Somerset Light Infantry and pursued a military career, but
it did not take me long to discover that I was too much of
a rebel to conform to the necessary disciplines demanded
of an army officer.

I moved on to politics, a profession that has never been
fearful of rebels.

May I take this opportunity of wishing you every success with your
book.

Best wishes

Yours Sincerely

Jeffrey Archer

The Mail on Sunday

Telephone: 071-938 6000
Telex: 28301

National Newspaper of the Year

Registered Office:
Northcliffe House, 2 Derry Street,
Kensington, London W8 5TS
Registered No. 1160545 England

4th April 1991

Dear Dominic Shelmerdine

Thank you for your letter of March 31st.

When I was a schoolboy my great ambition was to become a Member of Parliament and my ultimate dream to become Foreign Secretary.

I was motivated by the fact that in my youth Hitler had just become the Leader of Germany and was beginning a reign of brutality and aggression. I wanted very much to be in a position where I could oppose his politics.

But it was never to be.

When I did stand for Parliament after the War, as a Liberal, I was defeated at the Polls and became a journalist instead.

Kindest regards.

Yours sincerely

John Junor

THE MAIL ON SUNDAY LTD. (A subsidiary of Associated Newspapers Ltd.)

26

SCIMITAR FILMS LTD.

Directors: Michael Winner M.A. (CANTAB), John Fraser M.A. (OXON), M.Phil.

6-8 SACKVILLE STREET
PICCADILLY LONDON W1X 1DD
Telephone 071-734 8385
Fax 071-602 9217

4 April 1991

Dear Dominic,

Following your excellent persistence I am happy to write to you about my original ambitions in life. It was always my ambition to be a film director from my earliest memory. Around the age of four I remember giving a "film show" by making a shadow play with my hands on a white wall while another boy held a torch and I at the same time told a story to go with these shadow-images.

I remember later sitting on the toilet and a young girl was sitting next to me on a potty. It was a mixed school! I said to her "How did you like my film?".

She replied "I thought it was dreadful! I hate films, they frighten me."

So that was my first critic, met in a most appropriate place and in most appropriate circumstances.

All good wishes.

Yours sincerely,

MICHAEL WINNER.

THE FOOTBALL ASSOCIATION

LIMITED

Founded 1863

Patron: HER MAJESTY THE QUEEN
President: H.R.H. THE DUKE OF KENT
Chairman: F. A. MILLICHIP

Chief Executive:
R. H. G. KELLY FCIS

Phone: 071-402 7151/071-262 4542
Telex: 261110
Facsimile: 071-402 0486

16 LANCASTER GATE, LONDON W2 3LW

Our Ref: DB/6909   *Your Ref:*

5th April 1991

Dear Dominic,

Thank you for your letter of 2nd April.

I suppose my original ambition, in general terms, would have been to do some particular thing well. I chose a career in professional football and signed as a Grimsby Town player close to my eighteenth birthday. My ambition then would have been to make as useful a contribution as possible to the sport and to be respected by my peers as a good professional. It was much later that my ambitions became directed towards the managerial side of the game.

I confirm that I would have no objection to the above being used in your book.

Yours sincerely,

Graham Taylor
England Team Manager

Registered Office: 16 Lancaster Gate, London W2 3LW
Incorporated in London   Registration Number 77797

FROM: THE RIGHT HON. THE LORD PYM, MC

LONDON SWIA 0PW

5th April 1991

Dear Dominic,

From the age of fifteen it was clear to
me and my contemporaries that we were
going to have to fight a war. In my
case it was in a tank. My hope was to
survive the war and in due course,
later on, to enter the House of Commons.

These seem modest aspirations but in
the circumstances of those times there
was little choice.

Yours sincerely,

Francis Pym

From: The Rt. Hon. The Viscount Whitelaw, K.T., C.H., M.C., DL.

HOUSE OF LORDS
LONDON SW1A 0PW

7 April 1991

Dear Dominic Shelmerdine

Thank you for your letter
of 2nd April. When I was at
School and the University it was
my ambition to be a first class golf
player and to win Golf championships.
The war came in 1939 and changed
all that. Best wishes for your book.
Yours sincerely Willie Whitelaw

HOUSE OF COMMONS
LONDON SW1A 0AA
071-219 3405

8 April 1991

Dear Mr Shelmerdine,

Thank you for your recent letter.

My original ambition was to become a Journalist and War Correspondent, as was my Father before me.

Indeed, that is what I did for my first 8 years after leaving University at Oxford before entering Parliament in 1970.

Yours sincerely,

Winston S. Churchill

31

From: The Rt. Hon. Sir Edward du Cann, KBE

9 TUFTON COURT
TUFTON STREET
LONDON SWIP 3QH

April 9, 1991

Dear Mr Shackmundine

Thank you for your letter. I had no clearly defined ambitions as a boy except perhaps to play rugby and cricket for my school. I am glad to say I did both. I then became ambitious to pass my examinations so I could go to University. There again I was lucky. I passed them. I was in the Navy in the war. My ambition was to survive. I am glad to say I did that as well. When I was beaten in two Parliamentary elections, (as my father had been before me) I became ambitious to be elected for a West Country seat. I am glad to say I was elected 9 times. In business I was very keen to begin the revolution of a share owning democracy (in spite of much scepticism on my side of the House and the City establishment). Like many struggles those early days are forgotten now but they were a great adventure at the time.

Do I have any ambitions left? I have told my children I hope to live to a great age in order to be the confounded nuisance to them in my dotage as they were very occasionally to me in their youth!

9 April 1991

My dear P Marie

Thank you so much for your letter of 26 March. I am
flattered that you should wish to include me among the
hundred top people. I doubt whether you can use what
follows but it is an attempt at the truth. When I was at
my preparatory school I was regarded as a very clever
little boy and I assumed thereafter ~~I~~ that I would somehow
or other make my mark in the world. It was not however
until I got a 1st class degree at Oxford that my ambitions
took a definite shape. I wanted to be a politician but
a politician of no ordinary kind. While I was still at
school I spent much time in a boys' club run by my uncle.
When I left Oxford I was the only young Conservative with
any claim to call myself an economist. I gradually
therefore pictured myself as ~~xx~~ a social reformer whose
knowledge of economics equipped me to make sensible
suggestions ~~x~~ as to how the money could be provided. When
I was 30 I became a socialist, when I was 34 a Roman
Catholic. When I was 39 ~~axpxx~~ I became a peer and a junior
Minister. Even before that I had become a prison visitor.
So there you have it. Wordly ambition mixed up with
religion and a social commitment to the outcast. It is
certain that I have enjoyed much privilege. Success in
this world or the next is much more dubious.

Yours with very good wishes.

Frank

The Earl of Longford KG PC

Longford

THE RIGHT HONOURABLE

SIR LEON BRITTAN, QC

VICE-PRESIDENT OF THE COMMISSION
OF THE EUROPEAN COMMUNITIES

RUE DE LA LOI, 200
1049 BRUSSELS - TEL. 235 25 14
235 26 10

9 April 1991

D~ M~ Shelmerdine,

Thank you for your letter of 2nd April 1991, inviting me to write a letter to you about my original ambitions in life, for inclusion in your book.

When talking about one's early ambitions, you have to distinguish between real ambitions and ambitions which are no more than dreams. In the latter category comes the desire to open the batting for England. As an enthusiastic follower of the game, from childhood on, that was always one of my dreams. But my actual cricketing ability was so abysmal that this could never count as a real ambition.

When I first thought seriously about the matter, I decided, at a ridiculously young age that I might want to be a bacteriologist. I don't think I knew what it meant, but I liked the word, and had no doubt just learnt it. A slightly later ambition was to become an astronomer. That did derive from a genuine sense of curiosity, that wasn't well thought out.

At a later stage I became very interested in politics, but always thought that becoming a politician depended very much on luck, and that you had to have a proper career in any event.

Before going up to University I worked for a few months at the Oxford University Press, and seriously thought that I might want to go into publishing after my University studies.

But while at University, I was persuaded that my talents lay in the direction of the law, and switched over from studying English literature to law to see what it was like.

So I ended up as a barrister, but with a continuing interest in politics, sufficiently great for me to want to take up a political career if the opportunity arose.

The rest is in Who's Who!

Good luck,

Yours sincerely,

Leon Brittan

12th April 1991

Dear Dominic

I do thank you very much for your complimentary letter
and I'm happy to help with your compilation.

Actually I must be truthful and say I have achieved most
of my ambitions in life which I had when I was young, but
there always remains a couple of things one would like
to do before saying 'thats enough'!

And so here we go. I have adapted a short story written by
J.B.Priestly called 'Tober and the Tulpa' into a film script
that I'm quite certain could be the best film that I have
ever made. The subject matter is of Comedy,Horror,affection
for an animal. It has an acting scope that I would be proud
to take on. Unfortunately it has been turned down by a shower
of clever burkes who don't realise how good it could be nor
are they aware of the good clean entertainment that the public
would enjoy. Because the principal character is ageless, I
shall never give up trying. Wish me luck.

Yours most sincerely,

NORMAN WISDOM

TRANSPORT HOUSE . SMITH SQUARE . WESTMINSTER . LONDON . SW1P 3JB

TELEPHONE 071 828 7788 FAX 071 630 5861 TELEX 919009

Please quote our
reference when replying

OUR REF: RT/PM/MW   12 April 1991

YOUR REF:

Dear Dominic

In reply to your letter of 20 March, I cannot in all
honesty claim that I had any specific ambition in
my early childhood.

However, in my teens I developed a keen interest in
collecting fossils, an interest which I have retained
to the present day having built over the years a fairly
large collection.

Had my background circumstances and finance allowed
me any choice, it would have been my ambition to follow
a career in the field of pre-history.

Yours sincerely

General Secretary

General Secretary RON TODD   Deputy General Secretary BILL MORRIS

36

11 Venetia Road, London N4 1EJ

14th April 91.

Dear Dominic,

Thank you for your letter. My memory is not so wonderful
that I can be sure of my ' original ambitions 'quite a few
years ago.

At various time I wanted to be a train driver, a doctor and the
owner of the most wonderful sailing boat in the world. I did'nt
manage any of those and indeed,as I look back,my life does not look
very planned. I moved with events as they happened to me and have
travelled on a road I never expected... a very good one for all
that.
But if there was one'original'burning ambition in my twenties
it was to be a Catholic Priest and that ambition I did achieve
even though there also were problems I had never expected.
It was a worthwhile ambition. It brought me a lot of satisfaction
and I hope that , as a priest, I was of some help to others on
their own journeys through life .

Good wishes,

Bruce Kent.

THE RT. HON. LORD PRIOR   PC

17th April, 1991

Dear Mr Shelmerdine

        Thank you for your letter of 15th April.
Although I am flattered to be asked to take part in your
book, I am afraid that my remarks must be very brief.

        My first ambition was to marry and bring up a
happy family and to find a farmhouse and farm in the
countryside which would enable all of us to put down roots.
Political ambitions were not a foremost consideration in
early days, but I was given the opportunity of becoming a
Member of Parliament and this made it easy for me to deal
with a whole range of social problems for the many who
needed help. As time went on my ambitions widened and as a
Cabinet Minister there was an opportunity to influence
policy, hopefully for the good of the country.

        I always wanted to have a second career and was
lucky enough to have a chance of coming into industry,
which I believe has been sadly neglected. I now wish to
play some part in warning the Nation that unless
manufacturing industry is encouraged we shall all lose out,
and then to retire gracefully to the peaceful pastures of
the House of Lords and my farm.

Yours sincerely

Jim Prior

38

HOUSE OF COMMONS
LONDON SW1A 0AA

071- 219 4574

17th April 1991

Dear Mr Melmerkins,

Thank you for your letter of 16th
April. As far as I remember, my
original ambition was to be a Spitfire
pilot! Sadly, however, by the time
I had grown up, Spitfires were a
bit out of date.

BRITISH BROADCASTING CORPORATION
ON THE RECORD
LIME GROVE STUDIOS
LONDON W12 7RJ
TELEPHONE: 081-576 7927
FAX: 081-740 8549

18th April 1991

Dee Damian,

When I was a child I wanted to be the worlds best show-jumper.
A long time ago (1965) I became the South of Englands show-jumping
champion. Then I gave it all up. I still don't know whether it
was a good idea but I have to live with the consequences.

Yours sincerely,

Jonathan Dimbleby

FROM: SIR JOSHUA HASSAN G.B.E., K.C.M.G., L.V.O., Q.C., J.P.

57/63 LINE WALL RD

GIBRALTAR

18th April 1991

Dear Mr. Shelmerdine,

In reply to your letter requesting my original ambitions in life I would like to state that after the natural fantasies about the future during my early youth, once I was about to leave secondary education I made up my mind that I wanted to be a barrister and succeed in that profession.

Subsequently, I got involved in the development of the need for democratic institutions in Gibraltar of which there were scarcely any before the war. My ambition was that these should develop to a virtually autonomous government elected by the people for the people.

In the profession I got an honours degree, started law practice in 1939. I have done quite well. I became a Queens Counsel in December 1961 and I am the second senior practitioner in Gibraltar today.

In politics the urge to obtain self-government for Gibraltar after the war made me join others equally minded and we created a party which advocated advancement of civil rights and gradually obtained a municipality with a local elected majority which had not been the case before the war. Then a legislature with elected representatives entitling them to have a say in the laws to be passed, later to be expanded into what we have today which is a miniature Westminster pattern of Government and Opposition with elections every four years. This was the greatest ambition come true.

I took a prominent part in these events and was at the head of affairs in Gibraltar since 1945 until I decided not to contest the 1988 elections and retired in December 1987.

My other ambition was to have a family with children and as events have turned out I have been blessed with two families, two daughters from my first marriage now grown up and two daughters of my second marriage now studying and getting ready to go shortly into University.

Yours sincerely,

41

FULHAM FOOTBALL CLUB (1987) LIMITED

CRAVEN COTTAGE STEVENAGE ROAD LONDON SW6 6HH
TELEPHONE 071-736 6561
FAX 071-731 7047

19 April 1991

Dear Dominic

My original ambition was to be a professional footballer, would you believe? However, having won a scholarship to Henry Thornton Grammar School in Clapham and finding myself wearing school blazer, tie and flannel trousers, it soon became apparent to me that being a professional footballer was not considered a proper job by the school's careers master. So, on leaving at the age of 16 I ended up as a junior clerk in the London & Lancashire Insurance Company, moving a year later to the stock exchange and then at the tender age of 18 into the army.

In the army I found myself playing with professional footballers who taught me the basics of the game and when I came out two years later, third division Reading gave me a lengthy trial and to my horror didn't take me on, but fortunately second division Brentford offered me a contract at £7 a week in the winter and £6 in the summer. Thus my ambition was achieved, I was a pro, albeit a poorly paid one.

Yours sincerely

Jimmy Hill
Chairman

BRITISH BROADCASTING CORPORATION
KENSINGTON HOUSE
RICHMOND WAY, LONDON W14 0AX
TELEPHONE: 081-895 6611
TELEX: 265781
CABLES: TELECASTS, LONDON

EXTENSION:
DIRECT LINE:
FAX:

20 April 1991

Dear Mr. Shelmerdine,

I am not sure what my <u>Original</u> ambition was: probably
to stay alive. It still is. I can remember wanting to
be a world-famous sportsman. I didn't much care what
sport. I just wanted to be the best in the world at
it. Well, as you can tell, that one never get off the
ground. Somewhere around the age of 10 I decided I
wanted to be a newspaperman. I saw an American film
which made reporting look like a very exciting job.
This ambition WAS realised, although I found reporting--
and commentating--a demanding job and not nearly as
glamorous as that film made out. It didn't occur to me
at age 10 that the secret of a happy life was to find
a job you actually enjoyed. I stumbled on that by
chance. I've enjoyed working, which is probably more
than most people can say. But now the days of working are
running out. I just hope I shall be happy NOT working.

You may use this piece of nonsense in your book, and I
wish it great success.

43

NATIONAL VIEWERS' AND LISTENERS' ASSOCIATION

ARDLEIGH, COLCHESTER, ESSEX, CO7 7RH.
Tel: Colchester (0206) 230123
PRESIDENT:
MRS. MARY WHITEHOUSE, C.B.E.
GENERAL SECRETARY:
Mr. John. C. Beyer;
CHAIRMAN:
Mr. A. J. Hughes,
40 Fitzwalter Road,
Colchester, Essex, CO3 3SX
Tel: Colchester (0206) 45658

HON. TREASURER:
Mr. R. C. Standring,
Still Waters, Pine Walk, East Horsley,
Leatherhead, Surrey, KT24 5AG
Tel: East Horsley (04865) 2573

HON. MEMBERSHIP SECRETARY:
Mr. R. Silver,
50, Cherry Drive,
Royston,
Herts., SG8 7DL
Tel: Royston (0763) 241726

22nd April 1991

Dear Mr. Shelmerdine,

Tennis has always been my favourite game and, as a teenager I had an opportunity to play for Cheshire County – I lived in Chester at that time. Unfortunately, (!) I had just won a bursarship which committed me to become a teacher.

As it turned out I loved teaching and the work in which I have been engaged for the last 27 years sprang out of that!

However, I still watch tennis on TV whenever I can!

Yours sincerely,

Mary Whitehouse
President

London SW1

23rd April 1991

My dear Dominic,

    As a boy, I aimed to become a teacher. This, however, was not so much an ambition but a job which then appealed to me. But I soon realized that I was too impatient to be a good teacher.

    As a young man, one of my ambitions was to be a great QC, a brilliant and fashionable advocate, who earned enormous fees. But I only lasted little more than a year as a barrister. My ~~highest~~ ambition was to go into Parliament. I stood once, unsuccessfully. I was then aged thirty-five, after which I was too old to stand again.

    The one thing that I have never had any ambition to be is a notorious television interviewer. That just happened, by accident.

    So I have not done very well, have I? I suppose I've not really ever been seriously or ruthlessly ambitious. But thank you for inviting me to contribute to your book of ambitions.

Yours sincerely,

Sir Robin Day

45

Treasury Chambers, Parliament Street, SW1P 3AG
071-270 3000

29 April 1991

Dear Mr Skelmersdale

When I was very small, about twelve, my ambition was to be a Civil Servant, I rather fancied working in the Scottish Office. However, at various stages I thought I would like to be a politician - and then I thought, a journalist. Fortunately, I later decided to do something more worthwhile.

Yours sincerely

Norman Lamont

NORMAN LAMONT

TONY JACKLIN

golfscape

29 April 1991

Dear Dominic,

Thank you for your letter of 23 March 1991 and I hope the following information will be of some help to you.

My original ambition in life was to become a great golfer. As life progressed, my ambitions grew and my aim was to become the greatest golfer in the world which, for a short period of time, I possibly was.

May I wish you every success with your book.

Yours sincerely,

Tony Jacklin, OBE.

Tony Jacklin Golfscape (U.K.) Ltd.,
Quothquhan Lodge, Nr. Biggar, Lanarkshire ML12 6NB
Tel: (0899) 38183   Fax: (0899) 38125

ESTABLISHED 1791

THE OBSERVER

CHELSEA BRIDGE HOUSE · QUEENSTOWN ROAD
LONDON SW8 4NN · TELEPHONE 071 627 0700
TELEX 888963 · FAX 071 627 5570-2

From The Editor

30 April 1991

Dear Mr. Shelmerdine,

Thank you for your letter of 24 April.

My childhood ambitions did not crystallise until my teens, when I thought seriously (but briefly) of entering the Church. Then I wanted to fly with the RAF (an ambition I realised on my National Service). These early aspirations could not have lasted long, however, for the novelist Susan Hill, a family friend, clearly recalls hearing me say while I was still a student at Cambridge: 'I'm going to be Editor of The Observer'! That must have been 30 years ago.

Yours sincerely,

Donald Trelford

CASPAR WILLARD WEINBERGER
PUBLISHER

April 30, 1991

Dear Mr. Shelmerdine:

Thank you for your letter of April 17th, in which you tell me of the book you are compiling, and asking what my original ambitions might have been. I did not have any particular ambitions, but I have always felt that all people should participate in the operation of their government at some point in their lives. It just so happened that I enjoyed public service very much indeed, and consequently spent quite a number of years serving in that capacity in one way or another. I have found it very rewarding in every way, except monetarily, and I would highly recommend that more people become involved.

I hope this will be helpful, and of course, you do have my permission to include it in your compilation.

With best wishes,

Sincerely,

[signature: Caspar W. Weinberger]

THE GUARDIAN

ONE OF THE WORLD'S GREAT NEWSPAPERS

**119 FARRINGDON ROAD
LONDON EC1R 3ER**

Telephone 01-278 2332
Telex 8811746/7/8 (GUARDN G)
Registered in England No. 908396

Registered Office 164 Deansgate
Manchester M60 2RR
061-832 7200
Telex 668920 (evnews-g)

10th May, 1991.

Dear Mr. Shelmerdine,

Thank you for your letter. My childhood ambition was to play cricket for my county which, of course, I never did.

With best wishes,

Yours sincerely,

John Arlott

FRANKIE HOWERD OBE

18 QUEEN ANNE STREET

LONDON W1M 9LB

15th May 1991

Dear Dominic,

Thank you for your recent letter. It was my original
ambition when I was quite young and at Sunday School, to be
a Saint. However, the Church Warden recognised that I should
go on the stage and, as I thought it was the voice of God
speaking, through him I decided to follow his recommendation.
I am very glad that I did because as a Saint I would have been
a dismal failure.

With very best wishes.

Yours sincerely,

Frankie Howerd

JIMMY YOUNG

Broadcasting House,
London. W1..
15-5-91.

Dear Dominic.
Thank you for your
letter.
The answer is
boringly simple I'm afraid.
My original ambitions in
life were to be a musician
+ a broadcaster and, luckily,
I've been able to achieve.
Both.
Best luck with.
the book.

Jimmy Young

Gary Player
GROUP

May 15, 1991

Dear Dominic

Thank you for your letter concerning the book you would like to publish. Here is a anecdote that I feel reflects my original ambitions in life.

Looking back on my life and wondering about my original ambitions, I can't help thinking of an incident that happened during my school career. I must have been about fourteen at the time, when I found myself, together with a few friends, standing in our Principal's office. We had been caught playing golf during school time. There was no way out of the situation and we all knew that we deserved the punishment we were about to receive.

Our Principal was a man whom we all looked up to - he was a fair and sensible principal, however he had a difficult task of maintaining a high academic standard in an all boy's school. He spoke to us in a firm but gentle way. He was very pleased that we showed an interest in golf, as it was a game that he felt, developed strength of character, displayed qualities such as perserverence and determination, and most of all was a game that was almost impossible to master and thereby would be constant challenge. Surely, we were to take school more seriously, move ahead with our studies and become professionals to that we could secure our futures and become successful in our careers.

It was there in my Principal's office, that I believe my original ambition to be, not only a dedicated golfer, but a world class one as well. I have fulfilled my Principal's hopes, and have become a professional golfer and secured my future.

I feel that if you believe in yourself and show commitment to your interests, you stand a very high chance of becoming successful. I have lived out my original ambition, and there are fun things in life which are more rewarding!!

Yours sincerely

GARY PLAYER

GP/lett/016/gpg/lf

PO Box 785629 Sandton 2146   66 Rivonia Road Chistlehurston Sandton 2196
Telephone (011) 883 7220 Facsimile (011) 883 7250

375 NORTH CAROLWOOD DRIVE
LOS ANGELES. CALIFORNIA 90077

May 17, 1991

Dear Mr. Shelmerdine,

I was undecided about what to do
with my life until I was 21.

I had tried pre medical studies
at the University of California,
and although I was convinced that
I would make a fine doctor, I
could not jump the early hurdles,
mathematics in particular.

The alternatives, it seemed to me,
were journalism, globe trotting,
anthropology or creative writing
of some sort - short stories,
novels, poetry. I considered
spending my years as a pipe smoking
professor of literature, but that
would have required three years of
additional study and a doctorate,
after graduation from college.

Along came acting, in the form of
a college play. Once I propelled
myself out on the stage, half
paralyzed with fear, I liked it -
better than anything I had ever
done before. I performed, (or
tried to) in five plays during that
last year in college. The day after
my final exam, I took off for New
York City. Four years later I
landed on Broadway, and five years later
I found myself in Hollywood, where I
have toiled in the vineyards, so to
speak, for the past forty five years.

Yours sincerely,

Gregory Peck

DORIS DAY

May 18, 1991

Dear Dominic,

It was so nice to receive your letter,
and I would be honored to be included in your
book. You asked about my original ambition in
life and that was to be a ballerina. I was
enrolled in dancing classes from the age of
five, and ballet was my favorite thing. When
I was involved in a train wreck as a teenager,
my leg was severely broken in many places and
dancing was absolutely out of the question.
That's when I started singing.

My accident was unfortunate and certainly
not a pleasant experience, but it showed me
that what seemed to be a tragedy was eventually
positive and good for me in the long run. My
singing career was a most gratifying one, and
being able to communicate with song to so many
people was one of the loveliest experiences I've
ever had.

Thank you for thinking of me. I'll look
forward to receiving a copy of your book.

Most sincerely,

Doris Day

DD:jr

GEORGE McGOVERN
P. O. Box 5591
Washington, DC 20016
202/362-7052

May 21, 1991

Dear Mr. Shelmerdine:

Thank you for your letter of recent date.

With regard to my original ambition in life,
I decided as a high school student to become
a professor of American History. The influence
of my high school history teacher, Robert
Pearson, was the key factor in this decision.
He brought such passion, insight and imagination
to the teaching of history that it definitely
infected me at an early age.

I majored in history in college and then following
service as a bomber pilot in World War II, I
secured a doctoral degree in history from North-
western University. I served as a professor of
history for several years before my election to
the United States Congress.

Historical studies have continued to serve me
well as a public figure.

Sincerely yours,

George McGovern

2 ORME SQUARE
LONDON
W2 4RS

29th May 1991

Dear Mr. Shelmerdine,

Thank you for your letter.   I was interested to hear of your collection.

I had three alternative options which I might have pursued: the Chinese Art World;   I.T.V. and the Bar.   However, politics overtook them all and it proved to be an immensely worthwhile career.

With kind regards,

Yours sincerely,

[signature: Jeremy Thorpe]

JILLY COOPER

31st May 1991

Dear Dominic

Thank you for your nice letter. My
only ambition really in life is to
write books and for my family to be
happy and to have millions of dogs
and animals. It sounds an awfully
wet wish but I can't really think of
anything else. And I would like to
do something more positive to make the
lot of animals happier in the world
and also people, but I'm afraid because
most people look after people, I tend
to put animals first. Hope that will do.

Lots of love,

JILLY COOPER.

Speaker's House   Westminster   London   SW1A 0AA

4th June 1991.

Dear Mr Shelmerdine,

Please forgive me for not having responded to your letter, but I am overwhelmed with post at the moment, and it is extremely difficult to find time to give an adequate response to requests such as you make in your letter of the 13th April - and again on the 17th May.

The short answer is that I am blessed with having had very few ambitions, other than to seek to do any job which has come my way to the utmost of my ability.   Thus, when I entered my family business, Bernard Weatherill, my main determination was to ensure that the business, which had been started by my Father, after he had led a strike of tailors in 1912 in South Ascot, would become a household name.   To this extent it has, in that we now occupy the finest premise in Savile Row.'.

I was always determined to retire at forty, having made my fortune!   By 1960, I thought I had made my fortune, and the height of my ambition then was to become a Member of Parliament. I achieved this in 1964, and anything that has come my way since then has been nothing more than a bonus!

Yours sincerely

Bernard Weatherill

OCCIDENTAL INTERNATIONAL OIL INC.

123 BUCKINGHAM PALACE ROAD LONDON SW1W 9SW

TELEPHONE 071-828 5600 TELEX 739851 FACSIMILE 071-834 1752

6·6·95

Dear Mr Shenodin,

Thanks for your letter. My original ambition in life was to command the same regiment, The Royal Scots Greys, that my father commanded during the 39-45 World War & was killed in 43 as Colonel. I did not in fact fulfill my ambition but I tried hard!

Best wishes
Ranulph Fiennes

60

Georg Solti

7th June 1991

Dear Mr Shelmerdine,

Thank you for your letter of 29 May.

Since the age of twelve years, my ambition was always to become a conductor.

I wish you good luck with your book.

Yours sincerely,

Georg Solti.

14 Ladbroke Terrace
London W11 3PG.
12 June 1991

Dear Mr. Shelmerdine,
        Thank you for your letter of
May 29th.
        Because I grew up during the
Second World War my ambition — at
14 to 18 years — was the be a
navigator in the R.A.F. Basically,
anything to do with aviation was my
desire. At 17 I passed the air crew
selection board for the Fleet Air Arm,
to be trained as a pilot — not having
the educational qualifications to be
an observer — or navigator. I ended
up as a wireless operator in the RAF
for three years, so that in a way
was one ambition satisfied.
        Another ambition — related to the
first — was to be a radio officer in
the Merchant Navy, but nothing came
of that because of health reasons.
Then I had ideas of becoming a
land surveyor — but at that time
(or by that time) I also knew that
I had to become a writer. I
began writing at 20, and by the
age of thirty my first novel was
published.
        I hope this suffices.
        All best wishes,
        Alan Sillitoe.

62

19 June 1991

Dear Mr Shelmerdine

Thank you for your letter. When I was 17, my dearest wish was to be a writer. Now I am a writer, my dearest wish is to be 17.

Yours sincerely

USUAL ADDRESS   YELLOW COTTAGE
WALKING BOTTOM
PEASLAKE SURREY GU5 9RR

June 22 1991

Dear Dominic Shelmerdine

My ambition has long
been a simple one; I'd like my profession —
Composers conductors players singers librarians
orchestrators copyists pop stars backing
singers recording engineers, song writers lyricists —
to be in the forefront of a vast, severe
permanent outbreak of PEACE

Let all the above branches of the
lovely profession of music, and all the
participants, bend all their energies in this
direction + my most important ambition will
have been realized.

With best wishes

Harry Rabinowitz

26, MAUNSEL STREET,
LONDON, SW1P 2QN.
TEL: 01-828 1822

2nd July, 1991

Dear Mr Shelmerdine,

Although life is still busy, here is an attempt at answering your
two questions. Before doing so, however, thank you very much for
your generous gift of £10.

It depends what you mean by "my first serious ambition". If
you mean ambition for a career, then I think I have to say
that in my early days at University my general wish was for
a job that gave maximum excitement and interest, not too much
work and a good wage. Probably I wanted something with a
challenge as well. The war and service in the RAF, however
changed this dramatically. To begin with it gave me a
discipline, a sense of purpose and an understanding of the
value of tradition. What I knew what I could not achieve
on my own I found I could because you were a member of a team
and somehow you felt that other men had walked the path you
were walking and that in some real sense you were standing
in their shoes. You owed it to them to live up to their
example. When the war began to come to an end I realised
that I had a good chance of surviving, the thought that I was
one of the fortunate ones made me feel that I had a duty to
those who had not survived to make some sort of contribution
towards building peace. How, I had no idea at all, but, in
brief circumstances led me into the work amongst disabled people
that have been my primary job since then. Achievement, I have
come to realise from being with them, lies not in the achievement
itself but in what you have made of the opportunities, the talents
and the resources that God has given you. God has a plan for
each of us and the one thing that really matters is trying to
discover day by day what that plan is and fulfilling it to the
very best of one's ability.

Kind regards,

Yours sincerely,

Leonard Cheshire

BRIAN W. ALDISS

Phone: Oxford (0865) 735744
Fax: Oxford (0865) 326237

WOODLANDS
FOXCOMBE ROAD
BOARS HILL
OXFORD OX1 5DL

Mon: 22.vii.91

Dear Dominic Shelmerdine,

How ambition was born is not easily determined. To turn our memory back to the time of childhood is not as simple as some claim; we look back for logical reasons, but a child's mind is fairly anarchic and ruled, I believe, by many impulses other than logic.

From various causes, my concern in my very early years was with the question of survival, the basic ambition of living organisms! It would not be untrue to say that questions of mortality preoccupied me to a consuming extent, even at the age of three – certainly by the age of four. Perhaps this is why many of my stories reflect such concerns: fossils of an old anxiety.

Nevertheless, an ambition to express myself, to write and paint, sprang up, encouraged by external circumstances. At the age of four I entered a painting competition and won a handsome prize, a toy milk-float, manufactured by the now defunct Lines Bros. A more potent stimulus came about as follows.

When I had mastered the alphabet and first could read, I came across a story in the children's page of a national newspaper about a girl who lost her shadow. Her search for the missing shadow took her overseas. Eventually she found it in China. This story held some delightful and some sinister overtones for me. I was greatly possessed by it. It woke in me the urge to tell stories, stories divorced from everyday realism; also a wish to visit China – which I have done, and found it as magical a place as I hoped.

Very soon, I was making little fat books under my mother's tutelege, which she bound handsomely in pieces of wallpaper. From then on, writing became an inseparable part of life, and its great enhancer.

I began by saying that memories of childhood are untrustworthy. And, of course, writers are great embroiderers. But there's reason to be pretty certain of my facts here. Still preserved over the years is the letter announcing I had won the milk-float,and, amazingly enough, a picture cut from the newspaper illustrating the girl losing her shadow: coloured by me, in crayon, age four.

* * * * * * * * *

You'll see you've at last stimulated me into action! My trip to China was splendid, thanks; you'll see from the above why that country holds a particular mystic interest for me, though I found my shadow long ago.

I hope your book does well. Don't forget to send your contributors a copy.

All the best,

22.7.91

Dear Mr Shelmerdine,

Thank you for your letter of
July 17.

As you will see from my book, "Kill
the Messenger" I have had only one
ambition in life. That was to be a
farmer. Unfortunately I suffered from
almost every asthmatic allergy
under the sun, so I became a
journalist (instead of a geography
teacher, as planned). I have no
regrets, other than the loss of a life
in the open air, beautiful scenery and
communing with nature.

Instead, I have spent a working life
communing with life in a different
raw ———— politics.

I think I prefer nature — though
politics is nature writ large, without
the compensations of beauty.

Yours sincerely

Dominic Shelmerdine Esq,   Bernard Ingham

DEBORAH KERR

Switzerland

August 2nd. 1991

Dear Dominic,

Thank you for your recent letter - I shall be happy to
contribute to your book. My original ambition in life (aged
eight!) was to become a vet - but I soon changed my mind and
wanted to be a ballet dancer. Although I won a scholarship
to the Sadlers Wells Ballet School I soon realized that I had
started too late to study seriously. I also grew too tall
and I knew I would always have remained in 'the back row of
the swans'!

So...I became an actress, and it was a fortunate change
of direction for me!

With all good wishes,

Deborah Kerr,

Deborah Kerr

Sir Peter Imbert QPM
Commissioner of Police of the Metropolis

METROPOLITAN POLICE SERVICE

New Scotland Yard
Broadway
London SW1H OBG

30th August 1991

Dear Mr. Shelmerdine,

Thank you for inviting me to contribute to your proposed book in company with so many distinguished people.

I suppose that, like many people, my ambitions changed direction several times during my childhood and teens. For instance, as the son of a Kent farmer, one of my early ambitions was to become an agricultural engineer; another was to become a professional magician!

As I became older and thought about what I would do when I left school I had no strong views except that, whatever it was, I would do it to the best of my ability.

In the event when I left grammar school I became a junior clerk employed by a local council and my ambition at that time was to become a town clerk (now known as Chief Executives).

A year or so later however I found myself in the RAF for my national service and it was there that I realised my future lay in some form of public service and shortly afterwards I set my sights on the Metropolitan Police.

I do hope some of the above will be helpful to you in your most interesting enterprise and I wish you every success with your book.

Yours sincerely

P M Imbert

My first and burning ambition was to dance in the ballet. By 14 years of age I was heading on the large size, 6 ft plus 14 stone. So remembering the parable in the bible I developed my only real talent remembering the latin name of plants and I became what I am a Botanist

(signature)

Independent Television News Limited

200 Gray's Inn Road, London WC1X 8XZ

Phone: 071-833 3000

Direct dialling:

Telex: 22101 *Newsroom: News at One, News at 5.40, News at Ten*
266448 *Newsroom: Channel Four News*
268296 *Newsroom: Channel Four Daily, The World This Week*
269917 *Film and Videotape Library*

Cables: Telindep, London PS4

18 September '91

Dear Dominic Shelnerdine,

I'm sorry - but a complete oversight has meant I've failed to reply to your letter last May. It's probably too late now - but in case it isn't.

My original ambition was to become a doctor. It was an ambition which began when I was three, when my mother's brother - a gynaecologist - lived with us, in a room, at the top of the house for six months, during a course of study. I'd scuttle up to his room to admire the anatomy diagrams in his books and to gawp at the skeleton hanging in the corner. The ambition gradually faded in my teens, as I discovered I was quite squeamish. I finally went off the idea when I was sixteen and got better O level results in the arts than the sciences!

Good luck with your book.

Yours sincerely,
Leinath Boudawi

Registered Office: 200 Gray's Inn Road, London WC1X 8XZ. Registered number: 548648 England

GOVERNOR GEORGE C. WALLACE
P.O. Drawer 4419
Montgomery, Alabama 36103-5701
Phone (205) 241-9526

September 25, 1991

Dear Mr. Shelmerdine:

I have your letter of recent date regarding a letter from me to be placed in a book that you are compiling, and I am happy to accommodate you by sending you this letter.

I have had the pleasure of visiting the United Kingdom, and on my last trip there, (I believe it was in 1975.) I saw Prime Minister Wilson at Ten Downing Street where I had a conference with him for about 30 minutes. I also had a picture made but I have misplaced it. I also saw Mrs. Margaret Thatcher, who was the opposition at that time, and I have a nice picture of the two of us talking together. I always thought that she was a very fine Prime Minister and especially because she is so very friendly to the United States. However, Prime Minister John Major appears to be a real fine replacement as Prime Minister there in the United Kingdom.

With 95% of the people who live in the South--12 or 13 deep Southern states--if you pick up a telephone book in Montgomery or Birmingham, Alabama, you might think you have a phone book from London or Glasgow or some place there in your own country because the names are the same. My people originally came from, I believe, Antrim County, Northern Ireland. I visited Sterling, Scotland, where they have a big monument of Sir William Wallace. Whether I am related to him or not, I am not sure but my people came from Ulster and Scotland. My wife's name was Burns and mine, of course, is Wallace.

Of course, the United States and Great Britain have always been friends, and during World War II, they took a Gallup Poll before Japan attacked Pearl Harbor, and the Gallup Poll showed that every section in the country thought that we ought to stay out of this European war because they had been fighting each other for years and years and years and years. The only section that thought we ought to go to the defense of England was the South. Then they called us the Fighting South. I, of course, thought that we should have gotten into the war because of the great friendship that existed between us and also of the security it gave our part of the world with the Navy that you had in the

_____ Troy State University _____ Troy State University _____ Troy State University _____ Troy State University _____
Main Campus in Montgomery at Dothan in Europe

72

Atlantic and the one we had in the Pacific. However, after Pearl
Harbor people were very anxious to get into the war, and I did,
myself. I was in Law School at that time, and all of us in Law
School were afraid the war would get over before we could get in
it. But I got in in 1942 in the Air Cadet Program but I wound up
later on as a flight engineer on a B-29 Superfortress bomber
that had bombarded Japan almost into ashes. In fact, it's one
of the only wars we have won that we didn't have to invade the
country. It was won by air power alone. Of course, it had to
have the sacrifice of the lives of many thousands--some Army
units but mostly Marines who took the islands like Marshall Islands,
Mariana Islands, Iwo Jima, and I was stationed on Tinian in the
Marianas, and we flew missions from there night and day. We did
target missions in the daytime where we carried big 4,000 founders
and at night incendiary bombs that burnt down every city in Japan,
even those the size of 31,000. One incendiary raid over Tokyo
alone killed 80,000 people. According to Japanese authorities
who have written on this subject, so many people fled the large
centers like Tokyo that the war industries dropped to the point
where they could hardly do any work because of absenteeism.

This war is over, and even though Great Britain and the
United States and the allies won the war, we seem to have lost
the peace. We find Germany and Japan now the great economic
stronghold of the world. We are treated by the Japanese as if we
were the losers of the war.

I don't know what else to write but to say that I have
always had a great respect for the people of your part of the
world and thought that Winston Churchill gave the people so much
hope when he said, "We shall never surrender."

Again, let me say that I appreciated hearing from you, and
I hope this letter is some use to you in compiling your book.

With kind personal regards, I am

Sincerely yours,

George C. Wallace

GCW:hh

P.S. When I say 95% of the population are people from the British
Isles, we have a large black population which naturally originated
from Africa.

United States Senate

OFFICE OF THE REPUBLICAN LEADER

WASHINGTON, DC 20510-7020

December 4, 1991

Dear Mr. Shelmerdine:

Thank you very much for your interest in including me in your book.

One of my original ambitions in life was to be a doctor. I studied pre-med courses during my two years at the University of Kansas until December 7, 1941 -- Pearl Harbor changed many young Americans' plans, and soon I found myself in an Army uniform, heading to basic training.

During the Italian campaign, I sustained severe injuries in combat with heavily-entrenched German forces. In one shattering moment, my life had been changed forever. I realized I would never wear a surgeon's gown, much less practice medicine. In fact, the only challenge left for me was survival: getting off the battlefield, getting to a hospital, and then getting to know if I would ever walk again. It took 39 months in hospitals to begin my recovery. I did walk again, although I lost the use of my right arm.

While I struggled to recover, and while I learned to accept the truth about my disabilities, I decided to direct my energy towards helping people in another way -- public service. I saw it as a way to give something back to my hometown, my state and my country. I have never looked back. My career in public service has been a great and satisfying experience, and a reminder that despite disappointments and frustrations, life can bring unexpected rewards, so long as you don't give up.

Thanks again for your interest in my youthful ambitions, and good luck with the book.

Sincerely,

BOB DOLE
United States Senate
Republican Leader

VICTOR BORGE

Greenwich, Conn.
Dec. 26th, 1991

Dear Dominic Shelmerdine —

    In response to your request,
my original ambition was to do <u>every-
thing</u>!

    Would there not be time for
that, then I wanted to do the very
best allowed my abilities. And that
I have done ... and am still doing.

With regards,

STATE OF ARKANSAS
OFFICE OF THE GOVERNOR
State Capitol
Little Rock 72201

Bill Clinton
Governor

March 18, 1992

Dear Mr. Shelmerdine:

Thank you for your letter. I am happy to help you with your book.

At the young age of 16, I knew that I wanted to pursue a career in public service, and I decided to prepare myself for politics. Because government is so complicated, I set out to learn as much as possible.

Many things have influenced my decision to serve the people of Arkansas. My involvement in civic and political organizations when I was young sparked my interest in public affairs. President John F. Kennedy and Dr. Martin Luther King greatly inspired me to go into public service.

I have served as governor of the state of Arkansas 12 of the last 14 years. Prior to my gubernatorial election, I served two years as the state's attorney general. I am now 45 years old and am seeking the nomination to the Presidency of the United States.

I am committed to public service and believe that I have made a difference in Arkansas. I think that I would make a good President and hope I have that opportunity next fall.

Thank you for your letter. I hope that I have been helpful to you.

Sincerely,

Bill Clinton

BC:sw

FORTE

Hon. Rocco Forte
Chief Executive

RJVF/syh

27th March 1992

Dear Mr Shelmerdine,

Thank you for your letter of 5th March, and I am sorry for
the delay in replying.

I went to a Catholic School, Downside. Every year we had a
retreat. The retreat for the first year pupils was always
taken by Father (Hellfire) Blake, a Jesuit. He would
lecture us as a group and see us individually.

When I went to see him (I was 13), he asked me what I was
going to do. I said "Go into catering, Father". He
exploded. "Your father is spending all this money on your
education, and you want to go into catering!"

Things have changed, hotels and catering are now a
respected profession and the biggest employer in the UK.
I had already made up my mind then at 13 and never changed
it. I have no regrets!

Yours sincerely

Rocco Forte

Forte Plc 166 High Holborn London WC1V 6TT
Telephone 071 836 7744 Telex 264678 Fax 071 497 3094

Registered in England under number 76230 Registered Office 166 High Holborn London WC1V 6TT

1 Pennington Street, London E1 9XW *Telephone: 071-782 5000 Telex: 262139*

From the Editor

AN/MJ

12th May 1992.

Dear Mr. Shelmerdine:

My first real ambition was to become a movie director, though
since it was so unlikely I never mentioned it to anyone. I
wanted to make films about important subjects that would change
people's perceptions for the better. Instead, I ended up
editing a newspaper that tries to do that.

Yours sincerely,

Andrew Neil,
Editor.

27 May 1992

Dear Mr Shelmerdine

I am pleased to participate in your project.

As a young boy I became very ill with TB. I spent many
months in hospital. It was perhaps this that influenced my
great desire to become a doctor.

When I left school I was accepted by the Witwatersrand
Medical School but there were no bursaries available and the
cost was quite beyond the ability of my parents. I chose
second best as a career and decided to be a teacher,
there were few opportunities open to young blacks at that
time (sadly that situation has hardly changed). After
several years of teaching high school students, the
Bantu Education Act was instituted in 1955. It drastically
curtailed the freedom of teachers and the curriculum for
black students. I could not continue teaching under the
rigid, authoritarian conditions that gave blacks a "thin
gruel" of education.

I left teaching and entered theological college.

God bless you

Yours sincerely

Desmond Cape

"Beloved, let us love one another, for love is of God — if there is this love among you,
then all will know that you are my disciples."

79

HOUSE OF COMMONS,
LONDON, SW1A 0AA

3rd June 1992

Dear Mr. Shelmerdine,

Thank you very much for your letter about your project.

My grandfather and my father were Members of Parliament and a political career always interested me. However, while I was still an undergraduate at Cambridge, my father advised me not to try to go straight into politics. No-one, he said, will take any notice of you, since you will have no experience which would make what you say interesting. I took his advice, joined the Foreign Service and was a diplomat for 14 years. Looking back I am sure that my father was right. I left it a little late myself, and I would suggest that 35 is about the right age to start a political career. It has its ups and downs and its runs of bad luck, but it is a fascinating way of life. Politicians can handle a great variety of subjects and they have the opportunity to meet and sometimes help many different kinds of people.

Yours sincerely

Douglas Hurd.

Dear Dominic;

Whether it could be called an early ambition I cannot say
with any certainty I accepted at a fairly early age that my future
was to be as some kind of academic; My great grandfather when
he landed as an immigrant into Canada about the y ear
1800 registered as a teacher. We have no record of his academic
achievements before or after his coming to Canada.
My first advanced degree was in education, out of necessity as
a qualification for a teaching position. My principal
field of college teaching was in sociology, before that
was well defined or professionalized, and one qualified
to teach the subject if he had some knowledge of philosophy,
especially of ethics, and of history.

 I was studying for a doctorate in history when I
first became involved in politics and was elected to
the United States Congress. My involvement was quite
un-premeditated. Without the intervention of politics
I quite probably would have continued in the study and teaching
of history, principally that of the medieval centuries.

 I have been sustained in some of my writings by
the observation of Polybius that only politicians can write history
because they have been involved in its making, or words to that
effect.

 I have enclosed a bibliography.

Sincerely yours,

Eugene McCarthy

GLENDA JACKSON, M.P.

HOUSE OF COMMONS
LONDON SW1A 0AA

June 1992

Dear Mr Shelmerdine,

Thank you very much for your letter
and all your good wishes. My son
is doing extremely well and we both
appreciated your kind message.

As to my original ambition - I
wanted to be a ballet dancer, but I
grew too tall!

I hope this is useful for your book
and wish you every success with it.

Yours sincerely,

Glenda Jackson.

Glenda Jackson

24 JUN 1992

Dear Mr Shelmerdine,

Thank you for your letter of 25 May about the book you are
compiling. Your book sounds extremely interesting and it is a
great pleasure to be asked for my original ambitions in life.

I have to say that my real ambition, from the ripe old age of
seven, has always been to become a politician and a Member of
Parliament. On a lighter note my other driving ambition is to
be a jazz tenor saxophone player — one that I haven't been so
successful in yet!

I trust this will be useful to you and I wish you every
success with your book.

KENNETH CLARKE

Dominic Shelmerdine Esq

83

The Speaker

Speaker's House   Westminster   London   SW1A 0AA

2nd July 1992

Dear Dominic,

I don't normally reply personally to letters like yours because hundreds come into my office but yours is so persuasive that I shall make an exception.

When I was a small girl I wanted to be a window-dresser. It seemed a wonderful job to me. I knew where I wanted to work: at J and B, the big department store in Dewsbury, where I was born. I used to look in the store's windows and hope that one day I would be working there.

I certainly didn't think then that I would become a Member of Parliament and the idea of becoming Speaker never even occurred to me. But that's how things turned out and I don't suppose I shall ever be a window-dresser now!

With best wishes.

Yours sincerely,

SPEAKER

August 3, 1992

Dear Mr. Shelmerdine:

My earliest ambitions were influenced by a music conservatory and a public library located near my boyhood residence.

My parents believed that my brother and I would profit from pre-school piano classes at Jordan Conservatory of Music. At the ages of four and five, respectively, my brother and I were enrolled in a six-member class which progressed through lessons of rhythm, sight reading and actual keyboard instruction. I was excited by this opportunity and in the next few years began to improvise and then formally compose small pieces for performance. At the age of ten, my mother took me to visit the Dean of Music at Indiana University, a noted symphonic composer in his own right, and he encouraged me to undertake advanced composition.

At that point in my life, I could imagine a career as a concert pianist and composer. I read, eagerly, the biographies of famous concert musicians and composers of the past.

But about the time that this enthusiasm was reaching its peak, I began to visit the Rauh Memorial Public Library, located near our home, and borrow the maximum number of books allowed in each two week cycle. Most of my selections were biographies of famous people from many walks of life including musicians, but now moving toward kings, generals, American political figures, scientists, educators, and any other persons of note who stimulated my curiosity. As a boy, eight years of age, I had listened to the radio with my father, Marvin L. Lugar, and heard the radio broadcasts of the Republican National Convention of 1940 in Philadelphia. Wendell L. Willkie, a son of Indiana, was nominated on the sixth ballot in a most extraordinary turn of political history. By the time of the national political conventions in 1944, I listened and formulated with vivid imagination various scenarios in which I would be a participant in the Republican Convention, speaking to the delegates, and receiving their shouts of enthusiasm.

As my musical career progressed into study of the cello and many more group experiences in elementary and high school orchestras, my early ambitions centered on undefined roles in the political arena. I could not imagine the precise circumstances, but I knew that a life in politics would eventually be my calling, and I began to prepare for potential opportunities.

Sincerely,

Richard G. Lugar
United States Senator

RGL/hn

85

HOUSE OF COMMONS
LONDON SW1A 0AA

20th August 1992

Dear Dominic,

Many thanks for your kind letter and for letting me know about your exciting publishing venture.

As regards my own original ambitions I can well recall when at the junior school having the determined ambition to become a driver of one of Glasgow's wonderful trams. Sadly, by the time I became available for employment the trams had all disappeared and been replaced by buses and so I had to turn to some other form of employment.

I often wonder if perhaps I might not have achieved more in the business of keeping the country on the right tracks is I had been able to drive a tram instead of being involved in politics!

With all good wishes.

Yours sincerely,

Teddy Taylor

SIR TEDDY TAYLOR MP

Dominic Shelmerdine Esq.

Dear Dominic,

I am happy to contribute to your proposed anthology of ambition. It would be unsurprising to you when I tell you that my childhood and adolescent ambition was to compete at the Olympics. In 1976 I missed the Montreal Games by just one place in the 800m.

In 1980 at the age of twenty three I went to Moscow fulfilling an ambition which began in 1968 after having watched the Olympics of that year in Mexico.

I was indeed lucky in 1984 to get selected for the Los Angeles Games for my second campaign.

Yours sincerely

Sebastian Coe

From:
Lord Scarman

3/9/92

Dear Dominic Shelmerdine,

My ambition which led me
to the Bar was to become a
great advocate. My hero was
Marshall Hall, the great
defence advocate of the twenties.

Marjoribanks has written
a superb biography of this
astonishing man,

Yours ever
Leslie Scarman

CHAFFORD HUNDRED
ATHLETIC CLUB

5th September, 1992

Dear Dominic,

Thank you for your letter and I am obviously happy to contribute to your project with this letter.

I was twelve years of age when we were told the story of the Greek Goddess "Atalanta" at school. The image of a woman who could throw a spear further than any man captured my imagination, and I decided that I would be the best in the world at something when I grew up.

I had no idea at that time that it would be the javelin at which I would become the World Champion and World Record Holder.

When I first threw the javelin at my local athletics club, Thurrock Harriers, I discovered that I was quite good and I was told that I had a natural talent for the event.

Throughout my throwing career I remembered the Atalanta story and my decision to become the best in the world at "something".

I was delighted that it was the javelin that realised my dream!

Yours sincerely,

Fatima Whitbread

P.S. I have enclosed a signed copy of my autobiography which includes this information.

CLUB PRESIDENT
Fatima Whitbread MBE
Telephone: 0860 790369

Chafford Hundred Limited
Information Centre, Elizabeth Road, Chafford Hundred, Grays, Essex RM16 6QZ Tel: 0375 391099 Fax: 0375 391374

Pinewood Studios, Pinewood Road, Iver, Bucks SL0 0NH. Tel: 0753 630555. Fax: 0753 630393. Telex: 849577 Enigma G.

8 September 1992

Dear Mr. Shelmerdine,

Thak you for your letter about the book you're hoping to compile.

I'm in pre-production on my next film at the moment and, therefore, time will only permit me to write a short reply.

The first film I ever saw was the cartoon PINOCCHIO and I was so entranced by what I saw on the screen and the effect it had on me, that my ambition from that moment was to make films that filled people with the same feelings I experienced many years ago.

All the luck in the world with your book.

Kind regards,

Yours sincerely,

David Puttnam

DP/vk

Registered in England No. 1255496. Registered Address: 8 Baker Street, London W1M 1DA. VAT Registration No. 394 5275 19

HOUSE OF COMMONS
LONDON SW1A 0AA

The Office of the

Leader of The Opposition   11 September 1992

Dear Mr Shelmerdine

Thank you for your letter.

My original ambition was to be an advocate. I did
become a Queen's Counsel at the Scottish Bar but
politics intervened and I have become a politician
instead.

Yours sincerely

JOHN SMITH

1O DOWNING STREET
LONDON SW1A 2AA

THE PRIME MINISTER

14 June 1993

Dear Mr. Shelmerdine,

I was interested to hear about your compilation of 100 top people's original ambitions.

Mine were either to play cricket for Surrey, or become Chancellor of the Exchequer. In achieving the second I, sadly, failed lamentably in the first.

With best wishes for the success of your project,

Yours sincerely,

John Major

Dominic Shelmerdine, Esq.

The Rt Hon Paddy Ashdown MP

HOUSE OF COMMONS

LONDON SW1A 0AA

Our ref :- DAC/Ack/
Date :- 1 July 1993

Dear Dominic Shelmerdine

Thank you for your recent letter.

I think if I hadn't have become a politician, and if I had the skill and
ability, I would have liked to have been a musician. My son is a
musician and it is a gift which brings enormous pleasure.

Yours sincerely

Paddy Ashdown MP

MR CHOW

151 Knightsbridge SW1

July 6, 1993

LONDON   NEW YORK

BEVERLY HILLS

Dear Mr. Shelmerdine,

Thank you for the faxes.

Apart from birth, my first major adventure started at the age of 12 when I
left the comforts of home (Shanghai) to enhance my education abroad. I
suddenly found myself involuntarily independent in foggy London with food
rationing. Being Chinese I was presented with two options – laundry or the
restaurant.

After 25 years in the business and 10 restaurants later (with a few scattered
around the world and many ups and downs), the motivation has always been
the same. It is to keep the creativity flowing without repetition, keep
the boredom away from the dramas of life, and look for new inspirations.
One must seek for there is nothing else.

Sincerely,

周茨華

Michael Chow

P.S.   "By the way, do you know of any good laundy in town?"

MR CHOW
151, KNIGHTSBRIDGE
LONDON SW1X 7PA
☎ 01-589 7347
01-589 8656
CABLES CHOWCIAO

MR CHOW LA
344, NORTH CAMDEN DRIVE
BEVERLY HILLS
CALIFORNIA 90210
☎ (213) 278 9911

MR CHOW
324, EAST 57th STREET
NEW YORK NY 10022
☎ (212) 751 9030

7th July 1993.

Dear Dominic,

Thank you so much for wanting to include me in your book about People's Ambitions.

I have never really been a very ambitious person but, although my parents felt I should try and pursue a career in the theatre, before I left school what I really wanted to do was to go to university to study English. Unfortunately, in those far off days you had to have Latin to enter university and, although I had studied Latin until the age of fourteen (I was in South Africa at school during the war), when I returned to England the school I went to didn't offer this subject. So - I went to drama school instead!

Good luck with your book - I'm afraid the above information isn't terribly interesting!

Yours sincerely,

Virginia McKenna.

Virginia McKenna.

THE BORN FREE FOUNDATION, COLDHARBOUR, DORKING, SURREY, RH5 6HA, ENGLAND
TELEPHONE: (0306) 712091/713320/713431 FAX: (0306) 713350 REGISTERED CHARITY NO. 296 024
Director: WILLIAM TRAVERS *Trustees:* VIRGINIA MCKENNA, JOANNA LUMLEY, TERRY DICKINSON, BILL TRAVERS

ZOO CHECK, ELEFRIENDS *and* INTO THE BLUE *are projects of* THE BORN FREE FOUNDATION
Printed on Scandia Unique, a chlorine free paper from MoDo

27 May 1994.

Dear Dominic Shelmerdine,

Thank you for your letter of 19 May.

As a young person, I had a range of different ambitions. I remember as a 4/5 year old being asked what I would like to be and replying that I intended to be a Bishop. I am not sure where this came from and I am afraid that my religious phase didn't last long.

I then thought that I would be a lawyer, but always thought that sooner or later I would enter politics. I suppose it is fair to say that the factor that unites all of these various ambitions is that they all involve standing on my feet and talking!

Yours sincerely,

Bryan Gould

Virgin Management Ltd

120 Campden Hill Road, London W8 7AR
Tel: 0171-792 1371 Fax: 0171-792 3870

Our Ref: LC/DS/ed

7th June 1994

Dear Dominic Shelmerdine

Mine was originally to become a professional sportsman. Aged 10 I suffered a knee injury and had to turn my energies elsewhere.

As it's turned out, it was perhaps the best thing that could have happened to me since aged 40 I would have been unlikely to still have a job!
Kind regards

Richard Branson
Chairman
Virgin Group of Companies

Registered Office: 120 Campden Hill Road, London W8 7AR. Registered in England No. 1568894

9 August
1995

Dear Dominic,

"Original ambitions in life"? I can tell
you simply: When I was in my mid-teens, I was
pretty sure that God wanted me to be ordained.
How thankful I am that He led me in that
direction!

I was ordained at the age of 25, to + have
served God in the Ministry of His Church since then.
I am now 85. That work — as priest, bishop,
+ archbishop — has taken me all over the world.
I could want no greater calling. What better
task could there be that that of serving the
King of Kings?

Yours sincerely,

Donald Coggan.

FRISTON PLACE
EAST SUSSEX
BN20 0AH
EAST DEAN (0323) 422206

21 August 1995

Dear Mr Shelmerdine,

Thank you for your letter of 27 July. I am glad
you enjoyed the extracts in the Sunday Times.

As to your compilation - I had originally intended
to become a doctor, but because of my interest in
politics I decided to go for the Bar.

If this is of any interest, you may use it.

Yours sincerely,

[signature]

The Rt. Hon. Malcolm Rifkind, Q.C., M.P.

HOUSE OF COMMONS
LONDON SW1A 0AA

14 February 1996

Dear Mr. Shelmerdine,

Thank you for your letter with regard to your compilations of peoples original ambitions in life.

I am not sure that I can help you in this respect as I cannot recall any ambitions in my early years.

However, in my 20s I did consider that it would be very worthwhile to be a Member of Parliament and I am very pleased that this has indeed been possible.

With best wishes.

Yours sincerely,

Malcolm Rifkind

March 1, 1996

Dear Mr. Shelmerdine:

It sounds like you have a vast collection of ambitions! I wish you well in your compilation effort. Thank you for including me.

I have been fortunate to realize some of my original ambitions in life. Being raised in the heartland of America, I always wanted to serve my community and country as best I could. A number of opportunities for public service have permitted me to pursue this ambition.

I think I was able to help shape public policy in a useful way during my years in the U.S. Senate and working with President Carter during his administration. Although I did not grow up with a specific ambition to serve as Ambassador, I have found that this is also a tremendous opportunity for service to my country -- even if it is an ocean away from home.

With best wishes,

Walter F. Mondale

32A, OVINGTON SQUARE,

LONDON, SW3 1LR

TEL. 0171-584 1476

FAX. 0171-823 9051

2 April, 1996

Dear Dominic Shelmerdine

Thank you for your letter of 25 March.

When I was a small boy, I think I really wanted to be an ambassador, preferably in a very grand place! - the idea being that I could operate in the diplomatic world and represent my country in a way of which it could be proud. When I was young, quite a large proportion of the world was coloured red, so the situation was a little bit different from that of today.

With best wishes.

Sincerely

Carrington

Lord Carrington

2 April 1996

For Dominic Shelmerdine

When I was training to be a Doctor of Medicine I always wanted to serve the United Nations, possibly through the World Health Organisation. So I was very happy to have as my last job in public service the opportunity to co-chair, on behalf of the European Union, the International Conference on Former Yugoslavia with first Cyrus Vance, the former US Secretary of State, and then Thorvald Stoltenberg, the former Norwegain Foreign Minister, as the UN Co-Chairman. This experience made me even more committed to the Charter of the United Nations and determined to help make the UN more effective.

Yours sincerely

DAVID OWEN

Mr Dominic Shelmerdine

17 April 1996

Dear Mr Shelmerdine

In reply to your letter, my original ambition in
life as a young boy had been to study science as I
was particularly interested in the mysteries of
creation. However my father who was a distinguished
Rabbi was not happy about this and persuaded me to
enter the rabbinate. I come from a long line of
rabbis and my father wished me to continue this
tradition.

Later on I specialised in the subject of Jewish
medical ethics, and used this subject for my PhD
thesis, subsequently publishing it as a book. I
therefore satisfied my scientific interests, too.

I have never regretted following my father's advice,
as I have had opportunity and scope to realise all
my ambitions.

I thank you for inviting me to be included in the
100 top peope to be mentioned in your book, and I
hope that your endeavour will meet with success. I
look forward to seeing it in print.

With every good wish

Sincerely yours

Dear Dominic,
I hope this helps
Good Luck
Ross Ackland

Tel: 01237 431848

ROSS ACKLAND

The Old Rectory
Clovelly
Bideford
Devon
EX39 5TA

I never wanted to be an engine driver, or a soldier in a busby standing to attention outside Buckingham Palace. From the moment I first thought about the future I knew that I would be an artist of some description. It was an equally balanced choice – either painter, writer, actor or musician. The latter selection soon dropped by the wayside because we could not afford any lessons or instrument, although my great-aunt did leave us a pianola. But nobody really made it big as a pianola player. As I spent every second of my free time at the movies - legally and illegally - the idea of becoming a film director started to niggle away at my brain. Then when I was ten years old my father saw an advertisement in The Times 'Wanted twelve year old boy to play a leading role in 'On Borrowed Time' at the Haymarket Theatre. So, on a whim, I was sent along to audition with two hundred other boys. I knew nothing about the theatre – I had never been inside one. Maybe that is why I got the part. So I was given time off from Beckford Primary School in West Hampstead to rehearse at the Comedy Theatre. However the London County Council found out I was only ten, and everything stopped while the Court settled the matter. I was not allowed to do the play, so back I went to school. This did not upset me one iota, but the bug must have bitten because from that moment on I knew that I would become an actor.

During the war, when my school was evacuated to Bedford, I was offered a scholarship to the Slade School of Art, but a week before I was to take my matriculation exam I told my headmaster that I was going to be an actor and was leaving school. This confused him because I had never managed to get into any of the school plays - not even into the chorus of Cyrano de Bergerac. 'I feel I must warn you,' he said. 'I went to my tailor, for some new trousers, the other day, and he took more measurements than were actually necessary.' He paused impressively. 'There are a lot of people like that in the theatre.' I did not heed his warning and, at the age of sixteen, I hitch-hiked to London where I managed to get into the Central School of Dramatic Art free, because the war made them desperately short of males, and joined 'The Company of Tailors'.

Albert Reynolds, T.D.

Tel : 01-6183390
       01-6184210.
Fax : 01-6184199.

Church Street,
Longford.

April 18th, 1996.

Dear Dominic Shelwerding,

My original ambition was to

(1)   To become Leader of the Fianna Fail Party - the largest in Ireland and Taoiseach (Prime Minister of Ireland).

(2)   On becoming Taoiseach on the 11th of February 1992 I set out my two top Political Ambitions and Objectives

    (1)   To bring peace to Ireland by silencing the Guns on both sides.

    (2)   To Grow the Irish Economy faster than any of the Member States of the E.U. in order to create more job opportunities and a higher standard of living here.

Within 3 years the Guns on both sides have been silenced, the killing has stopped and Peace had come to Ireland after 25 years. (One of the Cease-fires has been temporarily breached).

The Irish Economy is growing at a rate 3 times faster than the average E.U. Rate of Growth and the highest ever rate of employment is now being enjoyed by our people.

Best Wishes.

Albert Reynolds T.D.

House of Lords

22nd April, 1996

Dear Dominic

    I was most interested to hear of your plans to compile a book about a "100 Top People's" original ambitions. I hope I can help a little by recalling two moments from my own early life, one during school days and the other from my time in the Army.

    One of my closest partners in the exploration of ideas and opportunities during my school days at Winchester was Robert Sheaf. Robert and I spent many days on holiday near his home in Guildford, at the beautiful Pilgrims' Way church of St. Martha's, drafting a political credo. The text - which we labelled the St. Martha's Charter - has long since been lost. But one idea on which we agreed was that I should become Prime Minister, while he would settle for First Sea Lord. As you will see, neither of us actually made the grade!

    A year or two later, as a cadet at the Mons Officer Cadet Training Unit in Aldershot, I was required, like everybody else, to write a single page essay on "My Aims in Life". I should guess that I was unique in restating my schoolboy ambition to become Prime Minister. Happily nobody seemed to take much notice of it, since it would scarcely have been consistent with the rating that I subsequently achieved in the unit boxing contest (which I had done my best to avoid): 'runner-up for best loser'.

    With every good wish for the success of the book.

Geoffrey Howe

"Die Anker"
Wilderness

29 April 1996

Dear Mr Shelmerdine

Since my university days I worked over a long period to become a member of Parliament, Prime Minister of South Africa and later State President of South Africa.

My interests are also concentrated on farming and nature conservation.

I trust this information will assist you with your project.

Kind regards.

PW BOTHA

/mh

OFFICE OF
THE CHIEF RABBI

735 High Road London N12 0US
Telephone: 0181-343 6301 Fax: 0181-343 6310

8 May, 1996

Dear Dominic,

My original ambition in life was to be an accountant. This was later displaced by a passion to be a barrister. Eventually, for two years, I became a professional philosopher. It was almost against my will, certainly against my expectation, that I then became a rabbi. It was, if you like, a vocation, a call, something I felt compelled to do. I felt that a generation of young Jews was being left without leadership and someone had to answer the need. I have never regretted the decision.

Yours, with best wishes,

Jonathan Sacks

Chief Rabbi Dr Jonathan Sacks

DAN QUAYLE

June 4, 1996

Dear Dominic:

Thank you for including me in your book. It is a great honor. Originally, I aspired to become a newspaper publisher. My father and grandfather were both owners and editors of several U.S. newspapers. In 1976, however, I was approached to run for the United States Congress, and the rest is history.

Good luck with your book. Please accept my best wishes for your continuing success. May God bless you!

Sincerely,

Paid for by Campaign America - A Multicandidate Political Action Committee (PAC)

HOUSE OF LORDS
LONDON SW1A 0PW

June 1996

Dear Dominic

Thank you for your letter.

My ambitions changed frequently. Having seen Ronnie Rooke, Fulham centre forward, score a brilliant hat-trick, I wanted to be Fulham centre forward.

Having watched Leary Constantine score a century and get the best bowling averages in the same cricket match at Lords, I wanted to be a test cricketer.

Having seen a moving film about a vet, I wanted to be a vet.

But it was at the age of 13, during the 1945 General Election, that I became fascinated by politics - and thereafter I always wanted to be a Member of Parliament.

Peter Walker

Please reply to 12 Cowley Street, London SW1P 3LZ
Tel: 0171 222 9695   Fax: 0171 799 2294

111

ELIZABETH TAYLOR

June 25, 1996

Dear Dominic,

Thank you for including me in your compilations conquest. You have asked me to share my original ambition in life, and so I will.

For as long as I can remember I had always wanted to be a ballerina. However, I suppose it just wasn't meant to be. Fate intervened and acting offers changed all other thoughts and plans--and viola! Here I am sixty-five years later a business woman and AIDS activist.

I hope you have enjoyed reading my original ambition just as I have enjoyed sharing it with you. I am delighted to have you include me in your book and am anxious to receive a copy.

Dominic, I wish you nothing but happiness and success in the years to come. Good luck with your book.

With affection,

Elizabeth Taylor

Dear Dominic:

"My first ambition was to be a Colonial Governor. I don't think plumes in the hat had much to do with it. The life seemed romantic, and in every other way suitable as well. Fortunately I grew out of that before we grew out of our Empire. Thereafter I knew that I wanted to be a Barrister, who in due course would enter Parliament in the Conservative interest and hold office. Being brought up to believe that I could achieve anything I really wanted to achieve, it had all seemed so eminently possible that I wasn't as surprised as I know I should have been when it came about".

Patrick Mayhew

Sir Patrick Mayhew QC MP
Secretary of State for Northern Ireland

HOUSE OF COMMONS
LONDON SW1A 0AA

26 November 1996

[handwritten salutation]

Thank you for your letter of 20 November asking about my early ambitions. One of my earliest ambitions was to become a musician but like many children I did not stick with it and I never came up to the standards reached by other members of my family.

Much later however, my ambition became more mundane and was that of becoming a successful lawyer. I was put off by not having the financial means or the family connections which in those days were pretty much a pre-requisite. The legal base nevertheless set me on my political path which I have followed since.

I hope this is what you were after.

[handwritten signature]

11 February 1997

Dear Mr Shelmerdine

I was not an ambitious child. I wished I could play the piano beautifully, like my brother Tom. But he was gifted, and I had no talent.

Yours sincerely

Diana Mosley

115

NIGEL HAVERS

24 February 1997

Dear Dominic

My original ambition was to be an actor and indeed it was not an easy ambition to achieve. Dedication, devotion and extremely hard work was and is required continuously and even with all of that an element of 'luck' occasionally does not go amiss.

However, the end results are highly rewarding and completely satisfactory and I am thankful now that my original ambition has been my only ambition.

Yours sincerely

Nigel Havers

NIGEL HAVERS

Margaret Thatcher

6 March 1997

Dear Mr. Shelmerdine,

When I was young, my original ambition was to join the Indian Civil Service, but when I discussed it with my father, he said, all too perceptively as it turned out, that by the time I was ready to join it, the Indian Civil Service would probably not exist.

At school I had always had a great interest in science, and chose to read Chemistry when I went to Oxford. It was a natural progression after University to take up a post as a research chemist.

Kind regards,

Yours sincerely

Margaret Thatcher

Dominic Shelmerdine Esq

THE RT. HON. THE BARONESS THATCHER, L.G., O.M., F.R.S.
HOUSE OF LORDS, LONDON SW1A 0PW

Stirling Moss Limited

14th March, 1997.

Dear Dominic Shelmerdine,

I am afraid my original ambition is rather boring as I had every hope and wish to be a dentist. I am glad to say it didn't work out and I became a racing driver.

My ambition may have been a little boring but I'm delighted to say my life certainly hasn't been.

Good luck with your book.

Yours sincerely,

Stirling Moss

46 SHEPHERD STREET LONDON W1Y 8JN   TEL 0171-499 7967 & 3272   FAX 0171-499 4104

Directors: STIRLING MOSS, O.B.E., F.I.E. V. K. PIRIE S. PAINE Registered Office: 35a HIGH STREET IVER BUCKS. Reg. No. 542345

SUSAN HAMPSHIRE

17th March 1997

Dear Dominic Shelmerdine.

Thank you very much for your letter. I think
my "original ambition in life"* is to survive
without hurting anyone. I hope this is
sufficient for your book, and wish you every
success in the project.

With all best wishes

Susan Hampshire

* and I think added to that
to help other to "survive" too.

Hon Ian Douglas Smith G.C.L.M., I.D.
Box CY 1089
Causeway
Zimbabwe

24.03.97

Dear Dominic Shelmerdine,

I congratulate you on your contribution to history through your attempt to produce a book depicting the original ambitions of certain prominent people.

I grew up in a small town in a rural area of Rhodesia where most people were close to nature. It was said that I could ride a horse before I could walk. Cattle and crops were always in the background, and I was never without a dog by my side.

Without food, there would be no life. So to produce food was one of the most admirable pursuits. I cannot recall ever deviating from my desire to farm. There were diversions when I flew Spitfires in World War II, and obtained my degree at University, and then my excursion into politics. But contact with my farm has helped me to retain my equilibrium and normality.

Long may it continue.

My kind regards and best wishes

KEN DODD

Knotty Ash
Liverpool L14 5NX

April 8th 1997.

Dear Dominic,

Thank you for your letter of the 11th March regarding a book you are compiling about prominent people's original ambitions in life.

A childhood ambition of mine was to follow in my father's foot-steps and play the saxophone. Unfortunately, my sticky-out teeth were not in tune with this wish and I kept biting the end off the instrument. I modified my ambitions and diverted my energies to becoming a tap-dancing ukele player. This I succeeded in!

Best wishes with your book.

Yours sincerely,

Ken Dodd

Terry Waite CBE

The Pink House The Green Hartest Bury-St-Edmunds Suffolk IP 29 4DH

04 May 1997

Dear Dominic,

Thank you for your letter. As a boy I had a great ambition to travel and see the world. I'm pleased to say that this simple ambition has, in the main, been achieved.

All best wishes,

Terry Waite.

Telephone and Fax
+44 (0) 1284 830 005

email
terry@ pinkhouse.demon.co.uk

The Laskett,
Much Birch,
Herefordshire HR2 8HZ
Tel: 01981-540-056
Fax: 01981-540-800

3CC Morpeth Terrace,
London, SW1P 1EW
Tel: 0171-828-9244

June 6th 1997

Dear Mr. Shelmerdine,

My original ambition in life was to design for the stage. Alas, coming from an impoverished family this option was hardly open to me whereas reading History with perhaps school teaching in mind seemed a sensible proposal in the climate of the 1950s. But I have been fortunate. My theatrical bent has found expression in two national collections, in exhibitions, in writing about pageantry and in designing gardens. Also, I married the profession I most wanted to pursue. So it all turned out well in the end.

Yours sincerely

Roy Strong

Brian Mulroney

Montreal, July 9, 1997

Dear Mr. Dominic Shelmerdine:

From an early age I wanted to be a lawyer. I achieved that ambition and went to work at a large law firm in Montreal.

The law can lead one to other careers and did in my case as well. It was a natural progression from law to politics and then, after serving as Prime Minister, back again to the same firm where I first began to practice as a very young man, many years ago.

Yours sincerely,

[signature]

OTTO von HABSBURG
Mitglied des
Europäischen Parlaments

Pöcking, 18 July 1997

My dear Mr. Dominic Shelmerdine,

My ambition in life, especially in the latest stages, is that the countries, which have been liberated from the Communist yoke, should be soon full members of the European Community and should live henceforth in peace and freedom.

Yours sincerely,

OTTO VON HABSBURG

Hindenburgstraße 15   82343 Pöcking   Telefon 0 81 57 - 70 15   Telefax 0 81 57 - 70 87   Telex: 5 216 640

DR. KURT WALDHEIM

Vienna, August 9th 1997

Dear Mr. Shelmerdine,

Thank you for your letter of July 29th, 1997.
You inquired about my original ambitions in life: I gladly inform you that my original ambition was to become a medical doctor. Later on I changed my mind and wanted to become a diplomat since it was my wish to get to know other people and to work for peace and international understanding. I´m glad that this wish was fulfilled.

With best regards

sincerely yours

Dr. Kurt Waldheim

+L.D.M.

MISSIONARIES of CHARITY
54 A, A.J.C. BOSE ROAD
CALCUTTA 700016 INDIA
24th August, 1997

Dear Mr. Dominic Shelmerdine,

Thank you for your letter, and your concern.

My desire to become a Missionary and
to serve Jesus in His poor became stronger
as I grew; and, I am grateful to Him
for using me, and giving me the Joy of
loving those He has chosen.

LET US PRAY.

GOD BLESS YOU.

M Teresa mc

National Party  *NATIONAL LEADER*

21 September 1997

Dear Dominic Shelmerdine

Although I have had an active interest in politics all my life, I have not always been a politician. For 12 years after I left University I was a successful attorney in the Transvaal town of Vereniging. I might have continued my career in the law. Just before I entered politics, I was offered the post of Professor of Administrative Law at my old university, Potchefstroom. Despite my love for the study of law, I nevertheless decided to embark on a political career.

With kind regards

F W de Klerk

F W DE KLERK

Pretoria P O Box 1692 Groenkloof 0027 Tel: (012) 344 6050 Fax: (012) 344 5286
Cape Town Private Bag X999 Cape Town 8000 Tel: (021) 461 5833 Fax: (021) 462 3008
E-Mail: fwdklerk@natweb.co.za

12.i.97.   Comedy Theatre
                      S.W.1.

Dear Dominic Shellerdine.
    Thank you for your
Kind Letter.
    My first Ambition in
Life was to be a
Classical pianist.
    Alas! I do not
possess the Required Skills.
            Yours Sincerely.
                Edward Fox

МЕЖДУНАРОДНЫЙ ФОНД СОЦИАЛЬНО-ЭКОНОМИЧЕСКИХ И ПОЛИТОЛОГИЧЕСКИХ ИССЛЕДОВАНИЙ (ГОРБАЧЕВ—ФОНД)

THE INTERNATIONAL FOUNDATION FOR SOCIO-ECONOMIC AND POLITICAL STUDIES (THE GORBACHEV FOUNDATION)

125468 г. Москва
Ленинградский проспект, 49
Контактный телефон: 943 9300
Факс: 943 95 94

49, Leningradsky Prospekt
Moscow 125468
Phones 943 9300, 943 9321
Fax 943 95 94

Дорогой Доминик!

Мои детские и юношеские годы пришлись на трудное время – война, тяжелый труд послевоеных лет. Откровенно говоря, в такое время не приходится о многом мечтать, кроме одной мечты – о мире, о нормальной жизни. Я помогал отцу, вернувшемуся с войны, работая помощником комбайнера, и далеко идущих амбиций у меня не было. Но можно сказать, что и тогда у меня была цель – честно трудиться, быть в числе лучших.

Я всегда хотел, чтобы моя жизнь прошла не зря, принесла пользу людям. О том, что получилось, я написал в своей книге, которую я Вам послал. Надеюсь, что ее чтение поможет Вам найти ответы на вопросы, которые Вас занимают.

С уважением

Михаил Горбачев

| МЕЖДУНАРОДНЫЙ ФОНД СОЦИАЛЬНО-ЭКОНОМИЧЕСКИХ И ПОЛИТОЛОГИЧЕСКИХ ИССЛЕДОВАНИЙ (ГОРБАЧЕВ—ФОНД) | THE INTERNATIONAL FOUNDATION FOR SOCIO-ECONOMIC AND POLITICAL STUDIES (THE GORBACHEV FOUNDATION) |

125468 г. Москва
Ленинградский проспект, 49
Контактный телефон: 943 9300
Факс: 943 95 94

49, Leningradsky Prospekt
Moscow 125468
Phones 943 9300, 943 9321
Fax 943 95 94

Dominic Shelmerdine
Fax: 44 171 370 ████

From: Pavel Palazchenko

Dear Dominic:

I am faxing President Gorbachev's letter to you. You will receive the hard copy later – it may take a little time. This is the translation:

Dear Diminic,

My childhood and adolescence happened to coincide with difficult times – war and the hard work of the postwar years. Frankly, in such times one does not have too many dreams, with but one exception – the dream of peace and of normal life. I was helping my father, who had returned from the war, working as assistant harvester operator, and I did not have far-reaching ambitions. One could say, though, that even then I had a goal – of working honestly and being among the best.

I always wanted my life to be not in vain, to be for the good of the people. What I managed to do I described in my book which I have sent to you. I hope that reading it will help you to find answers to the questions of interest to you.

Sincerely, and with warm best wishes,

Mikhail Gorbachev

United States Senate

WASHINGTON, DC 20510-2101

April 15, 1999

Dear Drum-Spelmardine,

Thank you for your letter and request for information about my ambitions in life. I am pleased to respond to your inquiry.

I developed an interest in politics at an early age. I grew up in a family where public service was highly regarded and where civil responsibilities took precedence over individual pursuits. At his inauguration, my brother, President John F. Kennedy, said, "ask not what your country can do for you – ask what you can do for your country." This philosophy continues to serve as an inspiration to me in my efforts as a United States Senator.

Again, thank you for writing to me. I wish you the best with your project.

Sincerely,

Edward M. Kennedy

6 FAIRHOLT STREET
LONDON SW7 1EG

0171-589 4291

23rd April 1999

Dear Dominic Shelmerdine.

Being of a considerable age, I find it difficult to recall my
original ambitions in early days. Nor do I think they were
clear-cut, largely because the situation in which we lived was so
uncertain – heavy unemployment and social unrest at home and
aggressive dictatorships on the Continent apparently bent on
war. You might have thought that survival would have been
sufficient aim but paradoxically the young are much less
conscious about survival than the old. What many of us
thought about, who were young in those inter-war years, was the
responsibility to try to avert such an unhappy and insecure
public situation in the future. It sounds priggish and I think that
there was a good deal of that in us. But they were not days of
unbounded pleasure and complacency.

I send you this with my best wishes.

Yours Sincerely,

Nicholas Henderson

SIR NICHOLAS HENDERSON GCMG KCVO

5 Park Road, Richmond, Surrey TW10 6NS

25.4.99

Dear Dominic Shelmerdine,

I wanted to climb Everest

David Attenborough

from Sir David Attenborough CH, FRS

DR. GARRET FITZGERALD

30 Palmerston Road,
Rathmines,
Dublin 6.
Telephone: 496 2600
Fax: 496 2126

5th May 1999

Dear Dominic Shelmerdine,

Further to your letter, I had two ambitions in life: To be engaged in the planning activities of our national airline, and to go into politics with a possible aim of becoming Taoiseach (Prime Minister). Both of these were in my mind when I was in my teens and I was lucky enough to achieve both objectives.

Kind regards,

Yours sincerely,

Dr. Garret FitzGerald

47A Heyman Road
Suburbs, Bulawayo
Zimbabwe.

May 24th, 1999

Dear Mr. Shelmerdine,

Thank you for your letter of May 14th and I am happy to give you the information you have asked for.

My family emigrated from Scotland in July 1867. For generations they had been brick and tile manufacturers and they established a factory at Waikiwi, Invercargill, in the south of New Zealand . having failed at farming.

I expected to follow in the footsteps of my father Thomas Todd who was Managing Director of the firm of Thomas Todd & Sons Limited.

However , at about 12 years of age I became interested in the Mission work of our Church in Southern Rhodesia. Anyway I worked with the Firm until 1927 when I decided to take the first step in my ambition to be a Missionary. I entered College and was ordained three years later as a Minister. In 1934 my Wife and I offered to go to Dadaya in Southern Rhodesia as missionaries.

For 20 years we worked at the Dadaya Mission and then I became the Prime Minister for five years.

Now, at 90 years I am living happily, with my wife in retirement at the above address.

I hope all is well with you,

Yours sincerely

Garfield Todd

The Hon. Sir Garfield Todd D.D, LL.D.

May 24, 1999

Dear Dominic Shelmerdine,

Thank you for your letter and your kind comments. Yes, you have my permission to include my reflections in your book. I look forward to reading it.

In answer to your query, my original ambition was to be an engineer running the steam engine, pulling a long train. As I grew older, I wanted to be a prolific writer and/or an athlete competing in the Olympic Games. Later, I developed an appreciation for extensive travel, public and foreign affairs and, making money! In my advanced years, what I would like most is to be strong and healthy until I fade away at 90+ - after a game of football with my great-grandson.

Good luck with your book.

Sincerely,

Douglas Fairbanks Jr.

30th June 1999

Dear Dominic Shelmerdine

Thank you for your recent letter about the book you are compiling.

My mother had become a widow in 1921 and had been left without any kind of pension. I had no particular ambition when the time came to leave school in 1929, but my mother was determined that I should not repeat her own very difficult life, and that I should find a job that would provide a pension when the time came for me to retire. As you can imagine, at my young age I was not very interested.

There was not much choice of jobs but at her insistence I sat for the Civil Service Clerical Examination and fortunately was successful. However, my own ideas developed in my late teens and I left the Civil Service after seven years.

Yours sincerely

James Callaghan

September 22, 1999

Dear Mr. Shelmerdine:

I apologize for the tardiness of this response to your July letter: I've only now returned from a film location in Spain which followed LOVE LETTERS in the UK.

I've wanted to be an actor ever since I was a child pretending in the woods of Michigan. I wrote a great deal about those and subsequent times in my autobiography which you might enjoy. I hope you can find a copy of IN THE ARENA and enjoy it.

Good luck with your collection as with all else.

Cordially,

1O DOWNING STREET
LONDON SW1A 2AA

THE PRIME MINISTER   16 November 1999

BY HAND

Dear Dominic,

Thank you for your letter. I am delighted to help with the book you are compiling.

On leaving school, I decided to study law at St. John's College, Oxford. My father, Leo, a qualified barrister, had a flourishing legal business and was always lecturing around the country, which influenced me greatly.

I was fortunate to fulfil my original ambition to become a barrister and sincerely hope that I will be fortunate enough to fulfil my present ambition, which is to win a second victory for Labour at the next Election!

With every good wish for your book.

Yours sincerely,

Tony Blair

Mr. Dominic Shelmerdine

JAMES A. BAKER, III
ONE SHELL PLAZA
910 LOUISIANA
HOUSTON, TEXAS 77002-4995

March 1, 2000

Dear Mr. Shelmerdine:

As a small boy in Houston, Texas, my first ambition in life was to be a fire engine driver.

In a sense I achieved that dream. During my years as White House Chief of Staff, Secretary of the Treasury, Secretary of State and campaign manager for three Republican presidents, I was often responsible for "putting out fires" -- in politics, in economics, and in world affairs.

Still, it would be fun to get behind the wheel of a big hook and ladder and turn on the siren!

With very best regards,

Sincerely,

James A. Baker, III

April 5, 2000

Dear Dominic Shelmerdine,

Thank you for your letter, your interest, and your persistence.

My earliest ambitions centered on athletics and I enjoyed participating in football, baseball, tennis, and golf. I liked the physical activity and competition, but I also liked the sense of being responsible in a team situation and accountable as an individual. My parents had high goals for me academically and encouraged me to do well in school. My father worked in Wall Street and early on I developed a keen interest in economics. Teaching on a college campus appealed to me. And after attending Princeton University and then serving in the U.S. Marine Corps during World War II, the idea of being of service to our government emerged. Although I have never run for office, I have been fortunate to be able to combine my interest in teaching economics with business activities and with government service.

I hope these few reflections are of interest. If you'd like to know more about my professional career, I suggest you read my memoir, *Turmoil and Triumph*.

With best wishes,

Sincerely yours,

George P. Shultz

The Daily Telegraph

1 CANADA SQUARE, CANARY WHARF, LONDON E14 5DT
DX42657 ISLE OF DOGS TELEX: 22874 TELLDN G
www.telegraph.co.uk

DATE AS POSTMARK

Alas, I had no ambitions in my early life.
When I was about 18, an influential uncle
secured me three interviews with prospective
employers: (a) Israel Sieff of Marks &
Spencer, (b) Sir John Reith of the BBC and
(c) Guy Pollock managing editor of the then
Morning Post.
The last-named offered me a job as a
reporter, starting the next Monday. 70
years on I am with the Daily Telegraph which
in 1937 bought up the Morning Post. That
today is called nepotism!

Best wishes,

5/127

143

Dr. Helmut Kohl MdB
Bundeskanzler a.D.

10117 Berlin, den 13. Juli 2000
Deutscher Bundestag
Unter den Linden 71
Telefon (030) 227 –73000/2
Telefax (030) 227 – 76840

Sehr geehrter Herr Shelmerdine,

nach dem Ende des Zweiten Weltkrieges, ich war damals fünfzehn Jahre alt und hatte eine große Zahl an Bombenangriffen miterlebt, wuchs in mir die Überzeugung, dass ich alles dafür tun musste, damit es nie wieder Krieg in Europa geben werde. Schon mit neunzehn Jahren, bei der ersten Bundestagswahl, habe ich für die CDU die ersten Wahlkampfveranstaltungen bestritten.

Später wurde ich in den Landtag von Rheinland-Pfalz gewählt, ich wurde Fraktionsvorsitzender der CDU und dann Ministerpräsident dieses Landes. Nach meiner Zeit als Oppositionsführer im Deutschen Bundestag wurde ich vom deutschen Volk zum Bundeskanzler der Bundesrepublik Deutschland gewählt. Dieses Amt hatte ich von 1982 bis 1998 inne.

In all den Jahren und bis zum heutigen Tag habe ich mich darum bemüht, meinen Beitrag zur Einigung Europas zu leisten, um meinen Jugendtraum zu verwirklichen.

Mit freundlichen Grüßen

Translation of Dr. Helmut Kohl's Letter

Dear Mr. Shelmerdine

At the end of the Second World War, I was just fifteen years old and had experienced a large number of air raids, I became increasingly convinced that I had to do anything to ensure that there would never be another war in Europe. When I was only nineteen, I led the first election campaigns for the CDU.

Later I was elected to the State Assembly of Rhineland-Palatinate, I became leader of the CDU party and then minister president of this state. Following my time as leader of the opposition in the German Federal Parliament, I was elected Federal Chancellor by the German people. I held this office from 1982 to 1998 inclusive.

In all these years and even to the present day, I have strived to contribute to the unification of Europe in order to turn my youthful dream into reality.

With best regards,
yours,
Helmut Kohl

N E L S O N   M A N D E L A
F O U N D A T I O N

01 December 2000

Dear Dominic

My original ambition in life was to become a lawyer.

Yours sincerely

M Mandela

NR Mandela

18th May 2001

Dear Mr Shelmerdine

In response to yours of May 12th, I can say that when I was
a boy, between the ages of 12 and 15, I wanted to be two things
in succession.   First I wanted to fly single seat jets in the
RAF as a fighter pilot;   second, I wanted to travel the world as
a foreign correspondent.

During National Service in 1956 and 1958, I managed the first
in Vampires and after three years apprenticeship on the Eastern
Daily Press in King's Lynn, joined Reuters and became a foreign
correspondent, which I continued for a decade until 1970 when I
wrote The Day of the Jackal and became a reasonably successful
novelist.   The third profession which has occupied the last
thirty years was one I never intended or envisaged when I was a
boy.

Yours sincerely

Frederick Forsyth

Helmut Schmidt

Dear Mr. Shelmerdine,

Thank you very much for your letter dated August 23.

My original ambition in life has been to become an architect and townplanner. But due to the fact that I had a small family and wanted to earn money as soon as possible I decided to study economics.

Wishing you a great success with your book,

Sincerely,

Alexander M. Haig, Jr.

September 6, 2001

Dear Mr. Shelmerdine:

Thank you for your correspondence and for your invitation to share with you some observations about my original ambitions in life.

As I wrote in my memoirs, *Inner Circles: How America Changed the World*, after discovering my father's World War I military uniform in his mother's attic, there was never the slightest chance, that I would be anything but a soldier. For a long time, no doubt, the intention was unconscious, but was always persistent: "I felt the pull of the adventure and excitement of the military life from the very first." Certainly the fact that the clouds of World War II were forming during my childhood contributed to this attitude.

My ambition was full-filled upon graduation from the U. S. Military Academy at West Point in 1947 and my commissioning as a second lieutenant. My military career culminated with retirement as NATO Commander in 1979. In war and peace it has been an honor to lead the men and women of America's armed forces and its allies. Service as Deputy National Security Advisor and White House Chief of Staff for President Nixon and U. S. Secretary of State for President Ronald Reagan were added honors.

Sincerely,

Alexander Haig

Hollinger

THE HON. CONRAD M. BLACK, P.C., O.C.
CHAIRMAN AND CHIEF EXECUTIVE OFFICER

TELEPHONE: (416) 363-8721
FAX: (416) 363-2454

September 7, 2001

Dear Mr. Shelmerdine,

Thank you for your letter. My original ambition, as I recall, was to be a considerably more influential media owner than I have any likelihood of becoming and to live in a house as grand and filled with valuable art and objects as William Randolph Hearst's home at San Simeon, California. There's not much likelihood of achieving that either, and my ambitions evolved. I don't feel I've done too badly, so far.

Best wishes,

Yours sincerely

[signature: Conrad Black]

September 9, 2001
0482/01

Dear Dominic,

I would like to congratulate you on your initiative to compile a book about prominent people's original ambitions in life, and feel privileged to add my own contribution to your collection.

I became involved with politics at age 16, and even then my ambition was to be instrumental in bringing the conflict in our region to an end.

I consistently wanted to see the Middle East enjoy a new era of peace and prosperity, and for the peoples of the region to coexist with one another, regardless of the differences between their background, religion and customs. I am optimistic that the day will come when this vision of better times will materialise, and the young generation will be able to look towards the future with hope.

Wishing you every success with your enterprise, and with my best regards,

Sincerely,

Shimon Peres

p+r=o+g=r+e=s+o   g+l=o+b=a+l

Felipe González

Sr. D. Dominic Shelmerdine

Madrid, 3 de octubre de 2001

Querido amigo:

En relación con su carta en la que me pedía le hablase de mis ambiciones, debo decirle que durante la dictadura de Franco quería recuperar la libertad y sentirme a gusto con mi pasaporte.

Esa ambición se fue convirtiendo en un deseo intenso de transformación de la realidad española. Gracias al apoyo mayoritario de los ciudadanos durante muchos años, ahora puedo decir que he contribuido al cambio y a la modernización de España.

Reciba un saludo muy cordial,

Gobelas, 31 28023 Madrid Tel: (34-91) 582 02 82 Fax: (34-91) 582 02 83 E-Mail: pnavarro@psoe.es

Mr. Dominic Shelmerdine

Madrid, 3rd October, 2001

Dear Friend,

Regarding your letter in which you requested that I talked about my ambitions, I have to let you know that during Franco's dictatorship I wanted to regain freedom and feel at ease with my passport.

That ambition grew into an intense desire for the transformation of the Spanish reality. Thanks to the support of the majority of citizens during many years, I can now say that I have contributed to the change and modernization of Spain.

With kind regards,

Felipe González

JUDI DENCH

25 January 2002

Dear Dominic Shelmerdine,

Thank you for your letter. My original ambition was to be a theatre designer, and that is what I started to train to do. However, encouraged by my brother (who was and is an actor), I switched to the acting course because it looked as if it would be more fun. I'm certainly glad I did!

Good luck with the book.

Yours sincerely,

Judi Dench

FAX & PHONE:
(011) 788-2833
INTERNATIONAL FAX & PHONE
27 - 11 - 788 - 2833
e-mail: helen01@icon.co.za

52 2ND AVENUE
ILLOVO
SANDTON 2196
SOUTH AFRICA

5ᵗʰ May 2002

Dear Dominic,

My original ambition in life was to become a lawyer and to fight many cases on behalf of wrongly accused persons or of persons whom the authorities were persecuting. Early marriage and World War II intervened, and having completed a degree in economics, I turned to politics. 36 years in the South African parliament opposing the apartheid government, gave me all the opportunity I wanted to learn law, and to use my position to exercise my original ambition.

Best wishes,

Helen Suzman.
(former M.P. South Africa.)

HOUSE OF COMMONS

LONDON SW1A 0AA

WH/sb

14 June 2002

Dear Mr Shelmerdine,

Thank you for your letter of 10th June and for enclosing a copy of the letter you sent to the Telegraph last year.

I have been passionate about politics from a very early age and have always wanted to follow a career path in Westminster. I have been a member of the Conservative Party since I was a teenager and hope to enjoy being a Member of Parliament for many years to come.

Thank you for writing to me.

Sincerely,

The Rt Hon William Hague MP

31, Walpole Street
London SW3 4QS
Telephone: 0171-730 2351
Facsimile: 0171-730 9859

26th June 2002

Dear Mr Shelmerdine

Thank you for your letter.

Until I was aged 22 or so I had no ambition at all in life except to do well in the Army; I was a regular soldier at that time. Then I became aware, while serving as ADC to a General based in Singapore, of the huge and fascinating strategic and foreign policy events going on around me. I decided at that time that the place to be was politics. From that time on my ambition was to become a Member of Parliament, which I succeeded in doing in 1966. Thereafter my ambition was very limited, although chance and good fortune took me into the Cabinet. In the last half of my life, all that I really wanted was sufficient money to retire comfortably and that has been achieved.

Yours sincerely

Sir John Nott

10 DOWNING STREET
LONDON SW1A 2AA

from Cherie Booth QC

26/06/02

Dear Bernie,

I have always tried to do my best and make my family proud of me. I would say that my ambition has been to make a difference & to better for my family, friends + country.

Yours
Cherie Blair

158

Bruxelles June 27 2002

Dear Quinine,

passions, like trees, grow slowly – One little step each year.

The same was for me.

This is the reason why I could be reasonably happy during all my life –

Con molta amicizia

Romano Prodi

LEVEL 19, WESTFIELD TOWERS
100 WILLIAM STREET
SYDNEY NSW 2011

8 July 2002

TELEPHONE (02) 93582022
FACSIMILE   (02) 93582753

Dear Dominic Shelmerdine,

At the age of 20 I contemplated becoming a school teacher.

Yours sincerely

Gough Whitlam

LENI RIEFENSTAHL - PRODUKTION
GOTENSTRASSE 13 * 82343 POECKING * FAX 49 - 8157 – 3569

15.07.2002

Dear Mr. Shelmerdine,

Thanks for your recent letter.

Concerning your request to find out my ambitions I would like to refer you to my memoirs (The Sieve of Time, London, Quartet Books). There you will find them very detailed.

In short terms my ambitions are:

- Dancing
- Climbing
- Mountaineering
- Diving

In the hope to help you with this I remain

sincerely

Leni Riefenstahl

arn ld palmer

post
office
box
fifty-two
youngstown,
pennsylvania
15696

July 15, 2002

Dear Dominic:

I was delighted to learn of the book you are compiling and would be happy to share with you my early ambitions in life.

Ever since the day my father first placed a golf club in my hands when I was a small boy, I had hoped to someday become a professional golfer. I immediately fell in love with the game and worked very hard to make my dream come true.

I consider myself very fortunate to have been able to reach the goals I set for myself and to make my living doing what I enjoy the most.

Sincerely,

Arnold Palmer

The Rt. Hon. Charles Kennedy, M.P.
Ross, Skye & Inverness West

HOUSE OF COMMONS
LONDON SW1A 0AA

Wednesday 17th July 2002

As a child, I was very interested in the space programme, having watched the fist lunar landing in 1969. One of my early childhood ambitions was, not surprisingly for a young boy at the time, to become an astronaut. At various other times I also toyed with the idea of becoming either a train driver or an actor.

As I grew up, my interest changed to politics and other, more academic subjects. I joined the Labour Party at the age of 15, and although I was shortly disillusioned, my interests in the political world remained, prompting me to join the Social Democratic Party, which later became the Liberal Democrat Party.

I feel that had I not followed this path into politics, I would most likely have become a journalist or a teacher.

Thank you once and again, and may I pass on my best wishes.

Yours sincerely,

The Rt. Hon. Charles Kennedy MP

Telephone: 020 7219 6226   Facsimile: 020 7219 4881
www.charleskennedy.org.uk

Telephone: 01246 582204
Fax: 01246 582937
Station: Chesterfield

24 July 02
Chatsworth
Bakewell
Derbyshire
DE45 1PP

Dear Mr Shelmerdine

Thank you for your letter — I am sorry to have been slow to answer.

There is no doubt that my ambition at the age of 12 ~ so was to work in a riding school and perhaps, one day, to own such an establishment.

That's all!

With best wishes

Yrs sincerely

Deborah Devonshire

Дорогой Доминик!

С большим удовольствием готов помочь Вам в составлении Вашей книги!

Моей первой мечтой в детстве было стать поэтом.

В годы Великой Отечественной войны я был сержантом – командиром советского танка Т-34. Лежа в госпитале после тяжелого ранения, я задумался над плохим вооружением солдат Красной армии, воевавшим винтовками против превосходящих технически сил фашистов. Моим единственным страстным желанием в ту трудную минуту было помочь своей многострадальной Родине одолеть грозного врага. Это привело меня к мысли о создании простого, надежного и мощного образца для простого рядового солдата. Всю свою дальнейшую жизнь я посвятил этому, чем занимаюсь и поныне.

С наилучшими пожеланиями в издании Вашей книги

Конструктор АК-47
Генерал-лейтенант

М.Т.Калашников

Dear Dominic!

Thank you for the letter. It's a pleasure to me to assist you in creating of your book.

When I was a boy my original ambition was to become a poet.

During the World War Two, I was a commander of a Soviet T-34 tank holding the rank of sergeant. Being badly wounded and recovering in hospital I figured out: Red Army was losing because our soldiers were insufficiently armed against technically completed Nazis. At that time I was possessed by merely one desire: to do something really useful to help our suffering Motherland to defeat the enemy. That ambition inspired me to design an automatic gun, which would be simple, reliable and effective and intended for the ranks. Since then I devoted all my further life to designing the guns and still working on.

With the best wishes in publishing your book.

Mikhail Kalashnikov

Lieutenant general,
Designer of AK-47

SIR JAMES R. MANCHAM K.B.E.

P.O.Box 29 Mahe Seychelles. Tel: 248 241717 Fax: 248 241545

E-mail: surmer@seychelles.net

18th August 2002

Dear Dominic

Thank you for your letter of 4th July 2002. When I was a young man the Seychelles was cut off from the rest of the world – a 1,000 miles from anywhere. There was no airport and we were visited only once a month by a steam ship which brought in visitors, mail and provisions from the outside world.

My first ambition was to break out of this isolation and make us part and parcel of the big world. Thus did I finally get an international airport for the Seychelles? Whether, seen in retrospect, this was the best thing for the Seychelles remains a debatable issue. My desire to see "progress" come to our "forgotten" islands propelled me into the realm of politics. Fifty eight years later a book entitled *The Sayings of James R Mancham* has been published in my native land. I am enclosing an autographed copy for you.

Thank you for your project and please do send me a copy of your book once it is published.

Best regards

Sir James R Mancham. KBE

Dick Francis

John Johnson (Authors' Agent)Ltd
Clerkenwell House
45/47 Clerkenwell Green
London EC1R 0HT

20 September, 2002

Dear Dominic,

Thank you for your letter.

When I was a boy my ambitions in life were to be Champion Steeplechase Jockey and to win the Grand National at Aintree.

I achieved the first in 1954 but, sadly, never the second even though I came close in 1949 on a horse called Roimond when beaten only by Russian Hero. I came closer still in 1956 when the Queen Mother's Devon Loch collapsed under me when we were well in front and with just forty yards to go to the winning post. I was never to fulfil that ambition but I cannot complain; I have achieved heights I would never have dreamed of, and my life has been varied, full and emotionally rewarding.

Yours sincerely

Dick Francis

House of Lords

6 October 02

Dear Dominic

When I was about fourteen years old I saw Eisenstein's great film 'The General Line' at Bradford Civic Theatre, and for many years thereafter my greatest ambition was to be a film director — I still perhaps hope to justify it one day

With best wishes

Denis Healey

Right Honourable LORD TEBBIT CH

House of Lords
LONDON SW1A 0PW

29 October 2002

D. Dummie

Thank you for your letter of 19 October
and your kind personal remarks.   I am glad
to say that I am fully recovered from the
indisp osition which kept me from the Foyles
lunch.

My early ambitions wavered a little.   For
a time I considered a scientific career in the
field of biology, then as my thoughts turned
to politics I decided I should go into the law
or journalism as a route to Parliament.

Since I could not afford to go into law I
left school at 16 to become a journalist.
— and then lost my way!

Norman Tebbit

MAIRIE DE BORDEAUX

Le Député - Maire

Nos références
DRI –MeG 1190

Date
13 novembre 2002

Cher Monsieur,

J'ai bien reçu votre courrier par lequel vous sollicitez ma participation à votre édition et c'est avec plaisir que j'y apporte ma contribution.

J'ai d'abord voulu être chirurgien mais, lorsque au cours d'un voyage en Angleterre justement, j'ai eu l'occasion de visiter une salle d'opération dans une clinique, ma vocation s'est très vite évanouie à la vue du matériel utilisé en chirurgie : scies, marteaux, vilebrequins, etc.

C'est sur les conseils de mon professeur d'histoire au lycée que j'ai décidé de préparer le concours de l'Ecole Nationale d'Administration (ENA). Ainsi, après une Agrégation en Lettres Classiques et un diplôme de l'Institut d'Etudes Politiques de Paris, j'ai pu entrer à l'ENA qui m'a beaucoup apporté dans mon parcours politique.

Je souhaite bonne réussite à votre ouvrage et vous prie d'agréer, cher Monsieur, l'expression de mes meilleures salutations.

Alain Juppé
Ancien Premier Ministre
Député-Maire de Bordeaux

Mairie de Bordeaux

Hôtel de ville
place Pey-Berland
33077 Bordeaux cedex

Tél. 05 56 10 20 30

Télex 550 007

Minitel
3615 Bordeaux
Accès Internet
"http://www.mairie-bordeaux.fr"

Town Hall of Bordeaux

The Deputy and Mayor

Our references
DRI –MeG 1190

Date
13 November 2002

Dear Sir,

I received your letter asking for my participation in your publication and I am delighted to make my contribution.

First I wanted to become a surgeon but, while on a journey in England, as a matter of fact, I had the opportunity to visit an operating theatre in a clinic and my vocation vanished very quickly at the sight of the instruments used in surgery: saws, hammers, braces and bits, etc.

It was after the advice of my history teacher at secondary school that I decided to go for the competitive exam for the National School of Administration (ENA). After graduating in Arts and getting a diploma from the Institute of Political Studies in Paris, I was able to enter the National School of Administration, which has helped me a lot in the course of my political career.

I wish all success to your publication and remain
Faithfully yours,

       Alain Juppé
       Former Prime Minister
       Deputy and Mayor of Bordeaux

STATE OF FLORIDA

Office of the Governor

THE CAPITOL
TALLAHASSEE, FLORIDA 32399-0001

www.flgov.com
850-488-7146
850-487-0801 fax

JEB BUSH
GOVERNOR

November 18, 2002

Dear Mr. Shelmerdine:

Thank you for your letter. I am pleased to contribute to your worthy project.

My original ambitions after graduating from college were to take advantage of our country's tremendous economic opportunity by working in the private sector, while raising a family and contributing to the community through public service. Above all, I believed that hard work would allow me to make a difference in the world in each of these areas.

I feel most proud of my family, although success is never final in either the Husband or the Dad business. As for my other original ambitions, I was initially very satisfied helping to run a small but dynamic real estate business in South Florida, while volunteering on behalf of the Republican Party in several capacities.

Over the years, however, I became convinced that Florida had even more potential than it had already realized, and that visionary leadership at the state level could make a difference in making sure that potential became reality. That's why I ran for Governor of Florida. After four years of hard work in the job, I feel that our team has indeed made a difference, though we still have a lot of work to do, and new challenges and opportunities present themselves all the time.

Life rarely turns out the way you expect, but if you have a vision and are willing to work hard to achieve it, good things happen. I hope your project is convincing you of that same truth. Good luck!

Sincerely,

Jeb Bush

Governor's Mentoring Initiative
BE A MENTOR. BE A BIG HELP.
1-800-825-3786

United States Senate
WASHINGTON, D. C. 20510

December 2, 2002

Dear Dominic:

Thank you for your letter. I appreciate your desire to include me in your book.

Upon graduation from South Dakota State University in 1969, I entered the U.S. Air Force as an intelligence officer. In 1972, I began working in Washington, DC as a staffer for South Dakota Senator James Abourezk. It was during that period that my ambition to enter representative government and serve the people of South Dakota took root.

In 1978, I ran for the United States House of Representatives where I served until 1986, when I was fortunate enough to be elected to the United States Senate. I have had the honor of representing South Dakota for 24 years. In addition, I have served as the Senate Democratic Leader since 1994.

I hope this information is useful to you. Good luck with your book!

With best wishes, I am

Sincerely,

Tom Daschle
United States Senate

Tony Benn
12 Holland Park Avenue, London W11 3QU
Tel: 020 7229 0779 · Fax: 020 7243 0009 ·(M): 0794 110 2163
e-mail: tony@tbenn.fsnet.co.uk

Dear Dominic

14 12 02

I wanted my chance to do good and resist evil.

And that means encouraging other people as they have encouraged me.

All the best

Tony Benn

U C L A
S C H O O L
OF PUBLIC
POLICY
AND SOCIAL
RESEARCH

DEPARTMENT OF POLICY STUDIES

January 13, 2003

Dear Dominic:

I'm sorry I have had to change the letterhead, but I teach every winter here at the School of Public Policy at UCLA.

I'm not sure I had any specific ambitions when I was young. I just knew that public affairs and having an impact on the world and the society in which I lived was something I wanted to do in some capacity.

Fortunately, I was blessed with the opportunity to do so as a legislator and chief executive in Massachusetts; and I almost had a chance to do it in the White House.

What more could one ask for?

All the best,

Michael S. Dukakis
Former Governor of Massachusetts

Bushey Park,
Little Newtown,
Enniskerry,
Co. Wicklow.

10th March, 2003.

Dear Mr. Shelmerdine,

Thank you for your letter of 15th November 2002 and apologies for the delay in getting back to you – this has been due to a heavy touring schedule.

In response to your request about my original ambitions, I suppose that like any teenager at the time, music fascinated me but because there was no history of music in my family to speak of, this did not seem to be much of an option. However, I was fortunate enough to be learning to play the guitar at the same time as bands like the Beatles and the Rolling Stones exploded onto the international scene supported by songwriters like Bob Dylan and Donovan. It was from these people that I learned to craft songs and enjoy singing as well.

It wasn't however, until I was in University that I realised that there was actually a chance to make a living in the music business, because prior to that, I had been completely unaware in my naivety that the music business could offer a career. I'm now glad that I pursued it as ambitiously as I have done! It's been a long hard road – things are never quite as easy as they look, but I have no regrets. Looking back, when I'm asked what else I would have done, my response has been, perhaps a job involving contact with other people, for example, the hotel business that my family were involved in, but it soon became clear to me that my true love was music.

With best wishes,

Yours sincerely,

Chris de Burgh.

HOWARD H. BAKER, JR.
AMBASSADOR

Tokyo, Japan

March 27, 2003

Dear Dominic:

I do appreciate your letter and I am deeply honored to have been included among your other friends who responded to your letter.

It is difficult indeed to identify my earliest ambition, let alone evaluate how it affected my life. When I was about eleven or twelve years old, I always thought I wanted to be an astronomer. World War II intervened and interrupted my ambition. When I was discharged from the Navy I realized I needed a more practical ambition. I finished college and became a lawyer.

I urge you on with your endeavor and wish you every success.

Sincerely,

Howard H. Baker, Jr.
Ambassador

12. 4. 03

Dear Dominic

Thank you for your letter enquiring about my earlier ambition. It was to become a radio officer in the Merchant Navy! As you know, I ended up in an entirely different communication business.

Yours sincerely

George Carey

4 Royal Park Mews · Vyvyan Road · Bristol · BS8 3AD
Email: glcarey@btopenworld.com

Piper Rudnick

901 - 15th Street, NW
Washington, DC 20005-2301
main 202.371.6000 *fax* 202.371.6279

SENATOR GEORGE J. MITCHELL
george.mitchell@piperrudnick.com
direct 6155 *fax* 6109

May 27, 2003

Dear Mr. Shelmerdine:

Thank you for your letter of May 20.

My original ambition in life was to be a professor of history at a small college or university. I attended such an institution - Bowdoin College in Brunswick, Maine - where I studied modern European history. My intention was to go on to graduate school to obtain an advanced degree and then to return to Bowdoin (or some place like it) to teach.

When I graduated from Bowdoin I entered the U.S. Army for a two-year tour of duty. During that time, my focus gradually shifted to the law. When I left the Army I entered the Georgetown University School of Law in Washington, D.C.

So I never truly fulfilled my original ambition. However I now occasionally lecture at colleges and universities and when I do I think about what might have been.

With best wishes.

George J. Mitchell

179

GARY LINEKER

10 June, 2003

Dear Dominic

Thank you for your letter of 3 June.

I always wanted to be a professional footballer or, failing that, a professional cricketer. If it had turned out that I was not good enough for either sport I would have opted for a career in journalism.

Having enjoyed a modicum of success in football, I have subsequently revived Plan C – journalism.

Good luck with your book.

Yours sincerely

GARY LINEKER

Joan Collins O.B.E

September 2003

Dea Dominic

Thank you for your letter, I'm afraid my ambitions do not have the same flair and excitement of Miss Day's and I hope they do not disappoint you.

As far as I can possibly remember, my ambition was always to become an actress and in later years to be a successful writer, both of which I thoroughly enjoy and am privileged to say have been relatively successful at. No great in depth story, they have been my ambitions.

When my daughter Katy was involved in a road accident many years ago, my sole ambition if you could call it that and the hope that she would pull out of the terrible coma she was in and to be healthy, beautiful young girl and thank God that ambition came true.

Wishing you every success with the book.

Yours sincerely

JOAN COLLINS O.B.E.

Lech Wałęsa

Szanowny Panie,

Dziękuję za list, który stał się inspiracją do refleksji nad przeszłością i własną drogą życiową.

Muszę jednak przyznać, że nie lubię patrzeć za siebie, bardziej zajmują mnie sprawy teraźniejszości i przyszłości. Zawsze podchodziłem do życia w sposób praktyczny, czasem aż do bólu. Liczy się dla mnie przede wszystkim działanie tu i teraz oraz jego konsekwencje. I to jest ta najprostsza, a jak się okazuje, skuteczna motywacja pozwalająca zmieniać świat. Wszelkie dodatkowe okoliczności przynosi życie, a rzecz w tym, żeby się dostosować i nie zatracić siebie, własnych ideałów. I to też mi się udało. A bywały różne etapy. Zaczynałem od budowania jedności, a po dojechaniu do przystanku wolność walczyłem o demokrację, pluralizm i podział. Zawsze jednak służę sprawom, pozostając wiernym sobie. Ocenę pozostawiam historii.

Lech Wałęsa

Pan
Dominic SHELMERDINE

Lech Wałęsa

Dear Sir,

   Thank you for your letter which inspired me to reflect upon my past and my own life.
   However, I have to admit that I do not like looking back, I'm more drawn by the present day and the future. I have always approached life in a practical way, often painfully so. The most important thing for me is to focus on issues here and   now, their consequences. This is the simplest, as it appears, motivation which lets   us   change the world.   All additional circumstances are brought in by life, the   point is to be flexible and   not to forget your own ideals and principles. There were various stages of life. I started from building unity and arriving at a point called freedom, I found myself fighting for democracy, pluralism and sharing.   However, being on duty, I have always remained loyal to myself. I leave judgment to   history.

                                            Lech Wałęsa

Dear Dominic,

"clue always
wanted to perform
or just plain act
up."

great good luck

love

Rivu

Leopoldo Calvo-Sotelo Bustelo

Alcalá, 93
28009 Madrid

Mr. Dominic Shelmerdine
London

Madrid, 2nd October, 2003

Dear Dominic,

While studying for my bacaularéat, I wanted to win the Nobel Prize for Physics. After completing my Engineering Degree, I aspired to design and construct large dams. Having become interested in politics during Franco's time, my hope was that the dictator would be succeeded by a Parliamentary Monarchy.

Neither the first nor the second wish were realized. The third one yes, although after a long wait. Later, I became a minister and then President of a Government (Prime Minister) under His Majesty, King Juan Carlos I.

Kind regards,

REPUBLIC OF ZAMBIA

OFFICE OF THE FIRST PRESIDENT

OFFICE OF THE PRESIDENT
PRIVATE BAG E501
LUSAKA
ZAMBIA

October 30th 2003

Dear Dominic,

    I wish to thank you most sincerely for your letters which I must say, made interesting reading.

    As a young boy, I was greatly influenced by my father David Kaunda, who was a Pastor at Lubwa Mission in Chinsali District of Zambia (Then Northern Rhodesia). Through his work, he made a great impression on me that I too wanted to become a Pastor. Unfortunately, he passed away when I was only eight years old.

    In later years, especially in the 1940s', the resistance movement against the colonial rule was steadily becoming more organized and intensified. I joined the Freedom struggle in belief that I would make a contribution to the attainment of independence of my country.

    I would like to say that although my original ambition was not fulfilled; I do not regret that, instead, I took up a different but equally challenging task of the liberation struggle of Zambia. For I believe it was a calling from The Lord Almighty God for me to serve HIS people in a different role from the one I originally espoused.

    I also believe that I did my best in the service of my country as a freedom fighter and as President. I wish to mention that it was an extremely humbling and rewarding experience in my life.

    I hope that this information will be of use to you.

    Wishing you God's blessings and guidance.

Sincerely,

Kenneth D. Kaunda
First President of Zambia

FRANK C. CARLUCCI

12/1/03

Dear Dominic,

From my earliest days in college I wanted to be a Foreign Service Officer, but my father urged me to go into business. I tried. I went to graduate school in business and worked for a company for a year. Then I quit and did what I really wanted. I was a Foreign Service Officer for 26 years and enjoyed every minute (the only FSO to serve as Secretary of Defense).

The moral - follow your heart.

Frank Carlucci

THE RT HON MICHAEL HOWARD QC MP

HOUSE OF COMMONS

LONDON SW1A 0AA

LEADER OF THE OPPOSITION

2 December 2003

MH/FHW

Dear Dominic

Thank you for your letter of 28th November and for your kind congratulations on my appointment as Conservative Party Leader.

I was very interested to hear that you are writing a book entitled 'My Original Ambition' and I am delighted that you thought to include me. I have to say that my earliest ambition was to play football for Wales – as you will appreciate a far cry from my present appointment.

I do hope you are successful with your book and I look forward to hearing of its publication.

With best wishes,

Michael

MICHAEL HOWARD

22 December 2003

Dear Dominic

Thank you for your letter asking if I would contribute to a book you are hoping to publish.

As a young person, I was influenced by what my father, who was a Congregational Minister, said, and that was "Belief in the fatherhood of God necessarily involves believing in the brotherhood of man".   My father's creed helped establish in me an ambition to always do my best and to contribute whatever talent I had to the betterment of my fellow man. Over my thirty five years in public life, in both the Australian Trade Union Movement and as Prime Minister, I feel I have gone a long way to fulfilling that early ambition.

Yours sincerely

R J L Hawke

Suite 1, 13th Floor, Westfield Towers, 100 William Street, Sydney NSW 2000, Australia
Telephone (02) 357 2444
Facsimile (02) 358 4162

189

JOAN SUTHERLAND

27th February, 2004

Dear Dominic,

You asked for a simple letter about my original ambitions in life.

All I wanted to do was to have the opportunity to sing at the Royal Opera House, Covent Garden. I never expected this would eventuate, or that I would have such a lasting career in so many of the other opera houses of the world.

I trust your book will be successful.

With good wishes.

Yours sincerely,

Joan Sutherland
OM, AC, DBE

Jean Chrétien, P.C., Q.C.

81 Metcalfe Street
Suite 700
Ottawa, Ontario, Canada
K1P 6K7

March 24, 2004

Dear Mr. Shelmerdine

It is with great pleasure that I reply to your letter and recall the following anecdote from my youth;

As a young boy living in rural Quebec, I was fascinated with civil engineering and wanted to become an architect. My father however, hoped that I would be a politician and raised me as such.

To ensure my success, my father suggested that I first study law and become a barrister, stating that it would then be easier to get elected.

I suppose he was right, as I have recently retired from a 40 year career as a parliamentarian and 10 years as Prime Minister of Canada.

I would like to take this opportunity to offer you my best wishes for success with your book, as well as in other future endeavours.

Sincerely,

The Right Honourable Jean Chrétien

Index